MIRROR & POOL

translations
from the Chinese

by
DAVID BURNETT &
JOHN CAYLEY

illustrated by
BRONWYN BORROW

notes and afterword
by JOHN CAYLEY

wellsweep

ACKNOWLEDGEMENTS

Cover design and illustrations by BRONWYN BORROW.
Calligraphy for the title page by JOSEPH S P LO.
Some of these poems have appeared in the magazines
Agenda, Numbers, and *The Patched Fool.*

Text copyright © Alfred David Burnett & John Cayley
Illustrations copyright © Bronwyn Borrow

First published in 1991 by
WELLSWEEP PRESS
719 Fulham Road
London SW6 5UL

0 948454 12 1   trade edition (laminated cover)
0 948454 62 8   readers' edition (laid paper cover)

BRITISH LIBRARY CATALOGUING-IN-PUBLICATION DATA
A catalogue record for this book is available from the
British Library.

Designed and typeset by WELLSWEEP.
Printed and bound by E & E Plumridge on recycled paper.

MIRROR

&

POOL

IN THIS BOOK twenty-eight Chinese poems are translated and adapted by one writer, then used as a point of departure by another. The poetic re-focusing of these distant images is further refracted and reflected in a set of torn-paper collages for twelve of the poems. The result is as stimulating an engagement with the problems and potentials of translation—in the broadest sense—as you are ever likely to read, or see.

DAVID BURNETT, until recently, a librarian at the University of Durham, was awarded a Hawthornden Fellowship in 1989. In addition to numerous professional, scholarly and critical contributions, he is the author of several collections of intense, lyrical poetry, the most recent of which is *Lesbos* (Tragara Press, 1990).

JOHN CAYLEY's translations from Chinese poetry have appeared in numerous magazines, most frequently *Agenda*. A collection of translations and original poems is forthcoming from Agenda Editions.

The illustrator, BRONWYN BORROW, has exhibited widely in the North-East of England and in London, where she now teaches. She is a painter who has also worked as a tapestry weaver, helping to bring a rich, painterly imagination to the craft.

AN AFTERWORD by John Cayley explains the background and development of the MIRROR & POOL project.

This image is coined by you,
My distant friend—

    Will you recall its shadow in a clouded mirror,
      Or know it better in this deep translucent pool,
      The creature of nature?

—Adapted from a fragment
by Bing Xin (1900–), number CXXXIX
in her *Maze of Stars* (*Fan xing*)

Contents

ALBA

'It is a cock that cries
The break of day!'

That sound in your ear is nought
But the hum of a dull fly.

'The east is light
And day is breaking!'

No light in the east
But the moon's rising.

Hush your busy insect's buzzing.
Another dream—with you—was sweet.

'Wake up and take your leave!
Don't make me hate you when we meet.'

Anonymous
From: *The Book of Songs*
(7th–8th century BC)

THE BLUE FLY

'Up! Dress! Away!
Already a cock crows
And dawn is bright as day.'
A cock? Or this? The night
Presses still, and blows
A blue fly to your ear.
'I tell you, a cock crows.'
A kiss may make you hear.
Dear, let me rest
For each dream is yourself.
You make two out of one.
'Can you not see the east?'
I'll give you east, and west.
— A girl's geographies
To have it back and faced.
'I tell you, it is east.
The sun knocks like a fist.'
Not east. 'Not sun?'
A moon bellied with that light.
'A tale like any man's.
You love my bed, not me.
Up, dreamer, and away!'
I'll stand you, girl, for this.
'Be off with you, at once.
I'll have you quarrel here.'
I'll give you quarrels, dressed.
A blue fly, do you hear?
'A cock.' Sucker! 'And yourself!
To come the moon with me.
I'll have you crow. Away!'

THE CYCLE

The rite is proven
As time is beaten.
The wand is passed
From dance to dance.

The slender girls,
Their songs
   which slowly drift and fade...

In spring the flower,
In autumn, fruit.
When shall it end?
Of old, forever.

Anonymous
From: *The Songs of the South*
(4th century BC?)

12

SPRING RITUAL

In the shaped, intricate dance
Each shuttles wands and sways
To the drum beat and chants,
A veiled violet, yet each gaze
Quickening a wild spring.

Chrysanthemums flower
At their feet, each shapely pace
A flux of silk and air,
The lissom, pure, and ancient grace
A rathe and ungathered spring.

Burial Song

Dew on a leaf
in an instant
dried.

Sun changed dew
shall shine
tomorrow,
shall fall
each dawn
and leaf
once more
be moist.

But shall a man
return
once dead?

Anonymous
(1st-2nd century AD)

The Shallot Leaf

Dew melts and sweetens to the sun
And each dawn glistens with a tear.

Dead after dead we weep and bear,
And change, and vacancy unknown.

After: An Old Quatrain

Haresilk follows a far wind
But root and stalk are still uncut—
If she who's loveless does not leave
How can he, in love, depart?

Anonymous
(1st–2nd century AD)

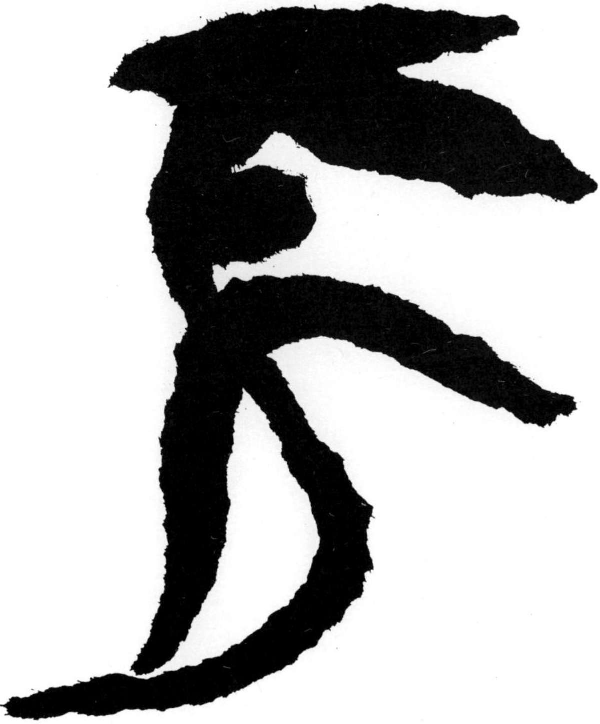

THE LOVE VINE

Mile after mile the wind
Drifts and trails with seed,
Yet root and stalk unbowed.

To feel nothing and remain.
And he to turn
Forever and stay still.

From: THE NINETEEN ANCIENT POEMS

The rushes, green
The willows, heavy
A lady at her window, sad.

A veil of white
A perfect face
A slender hand.

Once she played and sang for anyone
But then a wealthy suitor snatched her up.

Now he travels, will not hear of home.
Her bed is empty, hard to keep, alone.

Anonymous
The second of the famous
'Nineteen Ancient Poems'
(1st–2nd century AD)

ALONE

Willow chokes the stream
And each close, secret place.
And he thinks nothing
(For the green wine he tastes)
Of the wild greenness of her mouth
Or the green touch with men
Who is too made up and alone
And her heart (that is not his),
The lean, delicate desire
Unfastening each thought.

The Clear Dew...

The clear dew has stiffened to frost,
and flowers have all gone to seed.

Who says this 'gentleman' is 'worthy,
penetrating, successful'? —Can he

ride the clouds or summon the gods
or breathe the good air forever?

Ruan Ji
(210–263 AD)

THUS AND NOT THUS

Frost withers the bent grass.
Dry root and dry seed.
And these, who understand so much,
Their tongues that weigh gods, but indeed
Know nothing, and are loose as grass,
Wither, too, and how much.

HEROES

A fire which sweeps our plains
A torrent that drowns these shallows.

He hangs his bow on the tree of life
And rests his sword on the edge of the sky.

Everest is his whetstone,
A great river hems his robe.

When we consider Master Zhuang
How can we mention glory or decay?

His body abandoned in the wastes
Abused by kites and crows.

Was that not glorious?
Why then recall a hero's name?

Ruan Ji
(210–263 AD)

28

A Land Fit for Heroes

A bow hangs from the sun's tree,
Crooking the earth. The sky's extremity
A sword props. His scorch and tread
Stamp everywhere, raising the dead.

But, indeed, size hardly matters
And, at last, the stupefying shreds and tatters
That litter and bury weary acres
Crows pick, that soil with other, lesser ordures.

From: LINGERING CLOUDS

Still cloud, muffled weather
incessant, silent drizzle.
Everywhere the same dull light
and earth, a dull river.

No lack of wine. No lack of wine.
Enough to sip, and careless, watch the east.
Thoughts dwell on friends who will not come—
an empty road, an empty river.

Tao Qian
(365–427 AD)

CLOUD AND MIST

Autumn.
And all day
Banked swathes of teeming mist,
The cloud scarp steep as heaven.
Tenuity of light,
And the chill weight of air.

The nine heavens pent with cloud,
Fold gathered upon fold
And dragon fold of cloud,
The linked coils flattening beneath,
Thick, dull, and void as air.

Skyfolds possess us,
A blind emptiness.
Place vanishes
And a toiled fastness thickens,
A breath fastening each place.

Sky earths
And a wet blankness slaps the face.
Listening for friends,
With wine—oh, wine enough—
I pace from room to room,
Involved darkness,
Dragonish, and chill.

From: THE 'ZIYE' SONGS

'Courtship' thrives on upland meadows,
Brought down to the valley it passes for 'Matrimony'.
Or if you'd rather pluck some 'Love-in-idleness'
You meet your sorrow on an aimless journey.

Anonymous
From: The 'Ziye' Songs
(4th–5th century AD?)

CORK BLOSSOM

His mouth is a tall tree.
To walk always in its leaves!
And to lie down alone,
To find nakedness and no words.

What is so sharp as thorn
And bitter as the cork tree?
To brush nothing but the bloom
And to suck taste alone.

To shape the mouth alone
And pitch blossom of his tongue,
To sinew flesh and bone,
And eat the grass of words.

All day to walk like wind,
And to undress alone,
To learn nakedness as a wife
And taste nothing with the dead.

At Parting

Already the traveller
Broods within his heart,
Alone he sails
Another thousand miles.

Over the grey waters
With the rain about to fall,
The wind picks up
And the waves whiten.

He Xun
(d.c. 527 AD)

GOING TO THE RIVER

The spate darkened with impending rain
And white with wind. And you, at heart
Already far, a wild train
Of thought I cannot follow or depart.

A Complaint from Inner Chambers

Hushed and still, a hospice
    on the great north road,
Threading flakes of falling snow
    before a silken light.
Over the pond, the birds in pairs
    are never alone,
In curtain folds, the scent of 'Passion'
    curling senselessly.
An animate wind brushes the screen
    to bar the bright moon,
The pitiless lamp stays lit to shine
    on her sleeping alone...

'In Liaoxi, you said, the rivers froze
    and spring was brief.
Later geese came south, but still no word from you,
    on their long journey.
I wish you too would cross the passes,
    come back soon
To me. My beauty like the flower of peach or plum—
    falling petals of time.'

Jiang Zong
(518–590 AD)

First Snow on the North Road

Utterly silent,
The pass gorged with light.
A gray mass of air
A tower deathly still.

Nothing shuts out this cold.
In the close, shuttered rooms
The air's stillnesses, and light,
The scent of passion, silks.

At the frontier
The water hard as iron,
And spring only days.
Here, even here,
Already, the first snow,
At dawn, the walls' *sfumato*,
An empty, pitiless moon.

Already, beating south,
The pass heavy with their wings,
Geese thicken the dark air.
Is spring, is he so far?
One pulse so set apart?

To the tune: GAZING SOUTH

Don't cling to me
Cling to me, I'm much too fond of you.
You will break me
Break me off, I'm just a branch
Of willow which bends down
        over the river's song.

That man takes me, this man breaks
My heart. Can love be long?

Anonymous
From a collection of song words
unearthed at Dunhuang
(7th–9th century AD?)

Walking Both Ways

Come on, you know the score for tricks.
You can't think, surely, any care
Or die to kiss here and dip wicks.
You're lucky, fella. You can stare.

Come on. Besides, I fancy you.
Your girl now won't, or likely can't,
But any way with me you want
I'm game—try me. I'll show you too.

Come on! I'm crazy to get laid.
Is once all you want off with me?
What if you knock me up in bed?
Snake eyes! But just, do, please, kiss me.

Full Moon

The moon is out over Cold Mountain
    Round and alone.
It shines for all to see in the clear sky
    Empty of every thing.

It is given us. Then how shall we value
    A jewel without price—
This form reflected in every form
    And buried, deep in our flesh?

The monk Han Shan
(dates uncertain)

Moonlight at Cold Mountain

The full moon silent at the peak
And the world heavy with its light,
The changing to the changeless drawn,
And breath a vacancy of light.

CLIMBING CRANE TOWER

Last gleam of sunlight—
quenched on a shoulder of mountain,
Dull plumes from the soil-drenched river—
torn in the teeth of the sea.

Horizons which far-seeing eyes
first long to glimpse then gaze beyond,
Now urging footsteps on and up
another, further flight.

Wang Zhihuan
(688–742 AD)

CRANE TOWER

Climbing (and what stairs!),
Sky lengthens
And the river snakes to immensity.
A thousand miles
That fierce eye searching heaven!

Flight after flight of stairs,
And the sun dying,
Leaking from the air. Beneath,
Unemptying, remorseless, chill,
A damp ochre melts to sea.

man dreams

       cassia flowers fall

night stills

       spring mountains empty.

moon rise   startled   mountain birds

somewhen   singing   in spring streams.

Wang Wei
(701–761 AD)

MOONRISE

To walk asleep. Wild cassia,
And the hill a brim and sluice of blossom,
A sea of petals loosening their light.

Such stillness, and such vacancy.
In all the tangled knot of hills
One silence, and the stillness only,
A deep quiet sealed with streams.

Silence. And nothingness. In all the sky
The small, hard, empty moon of spring,
And a bird shrilling at such light.

SHADOW

Am I alone?
I seem to hear your voice...
    or echo?

I point out, as if to you,
    the ancient light
        which makes the mosses glow.

        So we return
        each evening
        to this hillside
        through the deep wood.

IMAGE

This evening, I can see
        the cold hillside
        and the setting sun.

I see those wanderers:
        ourselves
        alone.

The darkness of the wood
        we cannot enter.

Before us
    traces
        —not of men.

After: Wang Wei (701–761 AD)
& Pei Di (714– ? AD)

In Deep Woods

I

Silence, and emptiness.
The deer still as moss.
In these woods light
Chokes and every sound.

II

A hundred miles and more
Hill gathers upon hill.
You see deer, people never,
And tracks once or twice.

A mile away or more
Cones bristle under foot.
—That man, I wish him home.

III

Silences press in.
However quiet,
A word carries and breath rasps.
Always, in each place,
The deep stillness weighs.

Spring Awakening

Asleep in spring
I may not see the dawn
But everywhere
I hear the young birds' song.
Last night
Were sounds of wind and rain—
How many petals
Must have fallen down?

Meng Haoran
(689–740 AD)

SPRING WIND

All night to lie with wind,
The press and thresh of air,
And a boughed, spoiling light,
The peach doubled on itself.

To miss sleep, and sleep late,
The light shaken in each place
And a bird gathering its tune.
—How much has the air broken?

Jade Steps Complaint

Jade	Steps	Grow	White	Dew
Night	Long	Soak	Gauze	Stockings
Withdraw	Lower	Water–	Essence	Curtain
'Ling–	Long'	Gaze	Autumn	Moon

Li Bo
(701–762 AD)

CLAIR DE LUNE

The jade stairs glisten in the light.
Dew-mantled, her gauze stockings soak.
The swept veil's crystals clash and smoke,
Yet still she lingers stilled with light,
A gaze as still as moss or stone,
All autumn, trystless, and alone.

AUTUMN MOON

The air chokes with light.
The shock of white upon the steps,
And dew,
And her white stockings
Damp with waiting.

A curtain dazzles
As she turns within,
Pitch darkness,
And a tower of light,
And the light's silences
Alone.

AT PARTING

An old friend says farewell, leaving me
    To watch from upper floors.
Midst April's mists and flowers
    He drifts away toward Yangzhou.

The distant image of his sails—
    Their shadows faded into empty blue—
A long river flowing to the edges of the sky.

Li Bo
(701-762 AD)

Parting on the River Yangtze

I

Vanishingly small
Your sail thins to nothing,
A light doubled upon light.
Heart of my heart,
What are you now? And where?
Nothing remains. Only
Between us still
A pure light tall as sky,
The far river climbing heaven.

II

Stretching the sky
The slow, enormous light,
A silence moving heaven.

Without a tear or flaw
Mile after mile of light,
And a light moving upon light.

To see, and not to see.
To see, and see no more.
Only, a vacancy of light,
The river moving with its sky.

III

Unemptying sky
And the unemptied flow
Of water and pure light
One motion of all earth
And all of sky.

The bowed immensity of light,
And a light hanging upon light.
Far, far, and still,
A light for ever
Emptying ourselves.

IV

The last drop empties from the bowl.
Your sail vanishes at last.
Only the mist, and, always,
The far river meeting heaven.

SITTING ALONE ON
JINGTING MOUNTAIN

Flocks of birds
    fly up and vanish
Single clouds
    roll on, at leisure but alone.

While two of us here
    will never be bored
—myself and the mountain.

Li Bo
(701-762 AD)

BIG BROTHER

Two bald pates
Glisten to the sun.
Sagely I bow to it.
Imperceptibly
(As befits such eminence)
It bows to mine.

Between us
A world and its place,
The least breath in the grass.
—And that bird now
Skying your steep, beetled brow
To nod only,
Not kow-tow!

WRITTEN IN THE MEDITATION HALL
OF BROKEN MOUNTAIN MONASTERY

    Dawn clears
And enters the old temple,
    First light
Caught in the woods' tall boughs.
    A crooked path
Leads straight to the dark retreat
    Where monks just sit
Flowers and trees are deep.

    Mountain light
Blessed by bird song,
    Dark waters
Stilled in a man's heart.
    Here, the howl
Of nature is silent
    So only the tone
Of the soul shall sound.

Chang Jian
(8th century AD)

REAR MEDITATION HALL
BROKEN MOUNTAIN MONASTERY

A thousand years
Pine shingle and bowed eaves,
A roof shouldering the sky.
Hanging upon air
Sound falls to nothing here
A thousand feet beneath.

At dawn a hill of song
And the pure emptiness of light,
Each call a hill of light,
And the light singing in each place.

To the rear hall
You climb woods thick with blossom
And half a mile of air.
Here a world falls to shape.
You hear nothing, only
The bright stillness of the air
And a bell gathering its silence,
A sound emptying the sky.

The Round of the Moon

Still, alone, watching my window, full—
The river, cold, moving the night through my door—
As shifting flakes of light scattered on those waves
Or glowing from my silken mat—a pattern more sure—
As yet untouched by silent empty hills
While constellations fade where they are hung...

My old garden, where the pines are at their best,
Far distant, but within the perfect circle of this light.

Du Fu
(712–770 AD)

Full tilt and square upon the house
The sheer weight and press of light,
The latticed window rent and burst.
Within, a silk mat gleams and glistens,
Quicksilver flashes in the air,
And each wall shivers with the light.
Beneath, a shimmering snow, the water
Cannot settle; a toiled light
Troubles and unwinds. And, everywhere,
The sky-hung, enormous light
Flattening the caverned eaves and hills.
A thousand miles this water
And the broken light. You find it, too,
A pine's blackness and the brilliant air,
The unchipped, pure vacancy of light.

AT PARTING

A fullness which feels like emptiness,
A wine that brings no cheer.

The candle has a greater heart,
Shedding tears for us till dawn.

DU MU
(803–853 AD)

At Parting

The heart breaks,
And we say nothing,
Eat, drink, and say nothing.

Only the empty jug,
And a flame until dawn
Burns all itself.
The wax tears say all.

Overlooking the Lake: Drunk

Black clouds spill an ink
    which does not quite erase the hills,
Then hail dances in at the portholes
    stacked, and dishevelled.

Wind rolls the earth
    and scatters the weather,
Leaves us staring—at the water?
    at the sky?

Su Shi
(1037–1101 AD)

Not in Baedeker

Ink spills and blots but still, yet,
Stains but does not quite obliterate
The solemn round of sky and hills.
Hail drums the boards. Earth stumbles
Drunk as us and there, where you suppose
The muses' temple, a sheet flows.
A sun of smoking flax, the tide
Race quills and gravels, and each side,
Each which way, a wind barrels,
Slews, strains, shifts, shears and pummels,
—The 'whispering gale' the guide-book
Quotes and promises. Don't look
Beneath, but the sky (spewed, not purged)
Rounds on us like a squid disgorged.

To the tune: ZUI HUA YIN

Thin mists
    heavy clouds
  a sorrow which makes each day seem endless

(Fragrant camphor wastes away within
    a gilded animal).

When the feast of beauty
    should be shared again
Pillowed on jade
    within a veil of gauze
At midnight
    only fall's first chill
  will touch me.

I drink
    after sunset
  gazing east.

A lingering fragrance
    fills my sleeves with dusk.

Don't say
    I will not waste away
  with longing

(Lowering curtains
    against the autumn wind)

Already I'm thinner
    than this yellow flower.

Li Qingzhao
(1084–1155?)

Rust and sere yellows,
Thin mist and thickening cloud.
The petals shred and blacken
And a sun wastes to air.

Not the body
But a smell remains,
A memory of desire,
The scent ravelled in my sleeve.
Still, always,
In each place,
These shy propinquities.

I tremble at an edge of life,
A shadow, a dream's presences.
Feasts and rich hangings sicken me.
For all its gold each day
The camphor wastes to nothing
And I, too, with it.
Don't say I shall not waste with love.
I feel the sun,
I feel the rose in me.
That wind, that dead sun, trouble me.
Shutter the dark.

A DIVERSION after: Xin Qiji

I am young
and much too much in love
        with pleasure
to know anything of love,

And yet I force myself to tell
        of 'lyric' sorrows.

You are old
and they say
        (you hold your peace)
that you've been 'through the mill'.

Strange, you never seem to speak
        of anything but weather.

Xin Qiji
(1140–1207 AD)

A Cultivated Grief

Green, I wooed sadness high and low.
I lisped in numbers, and the numbers wept.
Now sadness courts me, —and I slow
To speak a rhymeless heart, except
'It is nice, isn't it, today?
An Indian summer, would you say?'

I'm not immortal, nor yet a Buddha quite.
　　Philosophy seems vague and distant.
But I know that I'm alone tonight,
　　Making this discontented moan.

The wind whirls the tumbleweed
　　Until its sad song is spent,
And mud that soaks the fallen catkin
　　Leaves a shallow blameless stain.

As I look down on nine men out of ten,
A hundred rightly label me a useless 'scholar'.

Don't say I bring it on myself
　　With mournful writings,
In spring, the birds, in autumn, insects
　　Make just such songs.

Huang Jingren
(1749–1783)

Sanctity? Hardly.
A vision, —a sublime
Nothingness at least?
What, then?

A habit of loneliness
And words.
Sunt lacrimae rerum,
And each dusk
The flux of words.

Dry thoughts in a dry season.
The spirit lists
And a dry scurrying persuades,
Raced tumbleweed and leaves.

For what?
Perdurable bronze?
A reputation always thin,
Ignorable,
Muddied, then failed.
The verse? A foolishness.
The long learning a fatuity.
Books? There are shelves,
A quantity of words.
A talent for sadness
(And sadness finds its own).

So, why words?
Only, the spring, scale,
Patterning and drift of song,
All autumn
This insistent churr.

LAKE ERHAI'S MOON

Wrapped in the wind of the passes,
Crossing the snows of Grey Mountain,
To cut a catchment in the hills...

Much later, moonlight covers a bedded lake.

From a contemporary folksong

Moonlight at Lake Erhai

At Snake Pass we wrapped the wind
About us, climbing to trench sky.
Tonight we wear the one coat,
Men and water, carrying the sky.

NOTES

Alba / The Blue Fly. This is ode number 96 from the earliest anthology of Chinese lyrics. Compare Waley's version in the *Book of Songs*, number 26, or Pound's in his *Classic Anthology*.

The Cycle / Spring Ritual. David Hawkes has made a complete translation of the important early anthology which contains this ritual song in his *Songs of the South*. It represents an exotic, southern, recognisably animistic tradition, very different from the northern Confucian orthodoxy.

Burial Song / The Shallot Leaf. Traditionally for the funeral of a prince.

After: An Old Quatrain / The Love Vine. 'Haresilk' is the literally translated name for a plant which has been identified as a form of dodder. A rootless plant, or rather one which loses its roots after twining parasitically around its host, the dodder trails in the wind and threatens to drift astray. Usual Chinese gender roles are reversed in our versions. In the original, both despite and because of their natures and tendencies, two differing plants remain entwined. In his final couplet the poet indicates that 'sensible' humanity might learn from the persistence of 'unfeeling' nature. The contrast, with its somewhat unconvincing admonition, has been more or less personalised in both the versions here.

From: The Nineteen Ancient Poems / Alone. Justly famous in English poetry for Pound's 'The Beautiful Toilet' in his *Cathay*, this is also the second of Waley's 'Seventeen Old Poems'.

The Clear Dew... / Thus and Not Thus. From 'Songs of My Heart' by Ruan Ji, a third century lyricist whose small corpus proved to be disproportionately important in the development of classical Chinese poetic forms. A complete translation has been published as *Wellsweep Chinese Poets 1*.

Heroes / A Land Fit for Heroes. 'Master Zhuang' is the philosopher Zhuang Zi (fl. 4th century B.C.) whose great, 'incomprehensible' book is, with the more famous, laconic *Dao de jing* by Lao Zi, the fountainhead of philosophical Daoism. Zhuang Zi is known for his doctrine of 'making things equal', a relativism which he invoked in order to put humanity and the world into proper perspective, and above all to give himself and his followers an imaginative understanding of their absolute freedom.

From: Lingering Clouds / Cloud and Mist. Part of a poem by Tao Qian corresponding to the second division of 'To-em-mei's 'The Unmoving Cloud" in Pound's *Cathay*. Waley called the same passage 'Flood'.

From: The 'Ziye' Songs / Cork Blossom. The original is a short quatrain from a collection of brief provocative verses full of pun and innuendo. The mirror version attempts to indicate the sort of tricks which are being played by substituting a few of its own. 'Courtship & Matrimony' is a Cumbrian name for Meadowsweet said to refer to its scent before and after crushing. The original imagery contrasts the 'sweetness' of lotus blossoms (a pun on love) with the real and figurative bitterness the cork-tree. The pool version has used this original imagery as its starting point.

Full Moon / Moonlight at Cold Mountain. Han Shan is famous amongst modern poets (especially the Americans) as the poet of 'Cold Mountain'. See the versions by Gary Snyder in his *Riprap & Cold Mountain Poems.*

Bird Song Stream / Moonrise. The mirror version here is literal and 'word-for-character', but is intended as finished.

Shadow & Image / In Deep Woods. We are now amongst poems of the Tang dynasty, the 'golden age' of Chinese verse. These versions are inspired by two poems. The first is part of a famous sequence by Wang Wei. His friend, Pei Di matched the sequence poem for poem and the second is his 'harmonising' quatrain. Neither version is a mirror to the original. This is, in part, because both writers have chosen to explore themes of their own which have been inspired by the original. A sensitive, poetic 'translation proper' already exists:

> On empty slopes
> we see nobody.
> Yet we can hear
> men's echoed phrases:

> Retreating light
> enters the deep woods
> And shines again
> on the green mosses.

> As the day fades
> see the cold mountain,
> Suppose us those
> travellers alone:

> We'd never know
> the deep woods' business
> But for traces
> of a stag or doe.

Translation by Arthur Cooper reprinted by kind permission, and published in Wellsweep's *The Deep Woods' Business.* For a brief and clear explanation of Chinese poetics along with many fine examples of sound and fruitful translation principles see Arthur Cooper's *Li Po and Tu Fu.*

Jade Steps Complaint / Clair de Lune & Autumn Moon. Here we have two pools and a single mirror. The mirror has despaired of adequately reflecting the original. Instead it shows one possible 'word-for-character' version. 'Ling-Long' is the modern romanisation of a so-called 'alliterative compound'. Here, it is onomatopoeic and suggests the quality of both light and sound as modulated by the 'crystal (lit. 'water-essence') curtain,' a door-blind made of crystal beads.

At Parting / Parting on the River Yangtze. Perhaps the most famous poem of parting, this is also Pound's 'Separation on the River Kiang'. The pool version has developed into an extended meditation on some of the images involved.

A Diversion after: Xin Qiji / A Cultivated Grief. Here, the mirror version is a free adaptation. For a clear reflection of a very fine poem see Arthur Cooper's version in *The Elek Book of Oriental Verse*, or Peter Jay's in *Agenda*, 20, nos. 3-4.

GENERAL NOTE: Romanisation of Chinese names is in the now standard 'Pinyin' system. A few common equivalents for initial consonants in the 'Wade-Giles' system will allow the general reader to match most of the poets here to names in, for example, Waley's various books:

Pinyin	Wade-Giles
b	p
p	p'
c	ts'/tz'
z	ts/tz
d	t
t	t'
g	k
k	k'
j/zh	ch
q/ch	ch'
r	j
x	hs

Thus, for example, Xin Qiji = Hsin Ch'i-chi and Ruan Ji = Juan Chi. This is a much simplified table of equivalent representations. There are further complexities but the above should be enough to confirm identities.

Afterword

SOME TIME AGO David Burnett attended a course I gave in Durham on Chinese poetry in translation. Along with a number of others, we studied and discussed various more or less famous translations and the original poems which inspired them. For each of the poems I also provided a bare, word-for-character transcription and encouraged everyone on the course to do their own literary adaptations based on their notes and our discussions. David is a fine, intense poet with many collections of his work in print. He produced a sheaf of striking versions which eventually formed the basis of this book. I had translated most of the poems he tackled and his adaptations inspired me to make up the complement. By now we had conceived the idea of a slender volume which would consist of our respective versions paired on the opposite pages of each opening. On the one side there would be my mirror-like version—most often a dimly reflective but conventional translation—and on the other there would be David's adaptation or variation, like a pool in which the images of the original were refracted and reassembled in what is at once a natural and an artistic process.

When all of the poems had been brought together Bronwyn Borrow was invited to consider the problem of illustrating them. After some experimentation she produced a number of black and white torn-paper collages which were lyrical, moving and restrained. They were abstract but contained suggestive elements of figuration which echoed and complemented images in the poems. They were not Chinese in style—although people who saw them claimed to detect a certain influence from the abstract formalism of Chinese calligraphy and they were monochrome like most Chinese ink painting—but they suited our versions well, and, in any case, the book was not intended as an exercise in Orientalism. We wanted it to be seen in its proper context and to be judged by the literary and artistic standards of the West.

Comparing alternative translations is always intriguing. It reveals the wide variation which is possible in versions which are nonetheless judged to be faithful by students of the original language. It also shows that although we may consider a particular translation to be good poetry, we may still find it impossible to square what we appreciate in the translation with either what native critics like about the original or what we may like about another, widely differing version. At least when we have more than one translation in front of us we can use them to perform, as it were, a literary and linguistic triangulation that may help to get us closer to the original than a single version in isolation.

I sometimes think—given the much-exercised and seemingly intractable problems of translation—that it might be better to ask not, 'Is this or that version close to its original?' but, 'Is this or that version close to some shared concern which the original poet, the translator and their readers all consider to be important?' This critical emphasis allows each party greater freedom of interpretation and makes possible a deepening and an enrichment of shared experience. It is also one of the few ways by which the translation process can be understood as working across different arts and media. The illustrations in our book have the same status and authority as any of the alternative literary versions. They are further complementary versions which translate a shared reading of selected poems in visual terms.

All of our interpretations are intended to be creative interpretations. Investing translations with a measure of new linguistic or artistic energy is the only way to render or 'give back' to a poem a measure of what, perforce, has been left behind. After all, what must be left behind is the original's very substance—the particular language of which it was made. We wanted our versions to have their own beauty, mystery and appeal. We wanted them to have their own artistic worth—enough to stand some chance of serving the intentions of the original poet better than an academic gloss. Our versions of the same poem differ significantly not for marginal or philological reasons, but simply because our capacities and interests are different. Our hope is that the images of these pieces will be further reflected and translated in the understandings of new and and even more widely differing readers.
                                                                    —JHC

96

BRIGHTON DIARIES

Memories of a Young Man in Peace and War

1929 – 1943

by

Ken Chambers

ISBN 0-9544299-5-8

Published by Hanover Books
www.hanoverbooks.co.uk
Printed by Lightning Source.

ACKNOWLEDGEMENTS

I am indebted to the Management of The Argus for consenting to the use of the three Brighton wartime pictures on pages 49, 105 and 144.

I am also indebted to Jennifer Drury for providing the picture of Ovingdean Grange.

I must thank my old school friend Bob Peters for his assistance in processing many of my photographs and my son, Nigel, for his help in the preparation of this manuscript.

Last but not least I thank my dear wife, Margaret, without whose help this factual history would never have been printed for she approved every page.

---

*This book is dedicated to my Cousin Cyril
– he will never be forgotten.*

CONTENTS

Illustrations

BRIGHTON DIARIES

Memories of a Young Man in Peace and War
1929 - 1943

INTRODUCTION

Covering the period 1929-1943 and written from diaries and memories, this history tells of Ken Chambers' life with a group of friends who grew up in the area surrounding St. Luke's Church, Queen's Park Road, Brighton. The story was motivated by an enduring great friendship between Ken and his cousin Cyril, until his life was cut short by the war in 1943, and is composed with him always in mind. While finishing the script Ken says he was reduced to tears as the memories of those latter months are still so real and painful. The original manuscript of just a few pages written 20 years ago, some five years after Ken's retirement, were recorded on cassette tape and copies sent to a small number of friends. A wartime comrade, Stan Hart, wrote back on 16th April 1991: *"Bless you dear friend, for sending me a copy of the lovely tape that you made, to your cousin Cyril. It is absolutely superb, perhaps the finest tribute I have ever listened to; spoken with such sincerity and depth of feeling; truly a precious friendship."*

April 2008

... a news cutting

KILLED ON 13th RAID

Sgt. D. Chambers.

A BRIGHTON airman who was reported missing over Germany a month after his marriage, Sgt. Douglas Chambers, of 54 Cobden road, has been reported killed he was shot down on his 13th bombing trip and his mother has been informed that he is buried in the municipal cemetery of Uden in Germany.

An old Brighton Intermediate schoolboy he volunteered two years ago, at the age of 19, and became a wireless operator air-gunner. Prior to the war he was employed as a clerk by the Brighton Co-operative Equitable Society. In May he married Corporal Rale Schaverien, ATS, of 24 St. Leonards Avenue Hove, and was posted as missing on 11th June.

PROLOGUE

The four engines of the heavy Halifax bomber were at full throttle as it raced along the runway and gradually lifted off the ground, up and away from RAF Station, Middleton St George, in Yorkshire. "A" for Able, of 419 Squadron RCAF (The Moose Squadron) was airborne, with a mission to bomb Dusseldorf on Friday, 11th June 1943.

There were eight crew members in the bomber, seven of whom had been detailed to fly together on twelve previous operations. The new crew member was W/O H.A. Tripp, the second pilot. More precisely, the other seven had flown together on eleven missions and not twelve, as on the first occasion which was an intended flight to Munich, on the 9th March 1943, the pilot, P/O W. J. Boyce, took off the aircraft without realising that his wireless operator was not on board. Boyce returned and circled the airfield, but could not land without first reducing the weight to the aircraft. He was duly instructed to jettison the bombs (probably over the North Sea), and use up sufficient fuel to bring the weight within the safety limit for landing. The missing wireless operator was Sgt. D.E.C. Chambers (1330903), my cousin Cyril, who had left the aircraft to go back and get his flight documents, unbeknown to the rest of the crew.

This incident was soon forgotten, but the crew were again frustrated on the following mission, which took place three nights later on the 12th March 1943. While on their way to Essen, the aircraft developed engine trouble and they were obliged to drop their bombs on a target in Holland.

Before the end of March, they had successfully attacked Duisburg and St. Nazaire, but were thwarted again on their first mission in April, when upon reaching the enemy coast while on their way to Essen, for the second time, engine failure forced them to return. Nevertheless, a further three raids were made in April without mishap; these were to Frankfurt, a long haul to the Skoda works at Pilsen in Czechoslovakia, and to the Baltic port of Stettin. Another four missions were flown in the month of May; all of these were to towns and cities in the industrial area of the Ruhr, which was being incessantly bombed and was heavily defended by ack-ack guns. This accounted for the fact that the Squadron had lost nine aircraft during the month, and two of those were crewed by airmen on their first operation.

3

It was now late in the evening of 11th June, and the Squadron was on its first assignment of the month. Seventeen crews had been briefed. One had failed to take off. Five had returned early. The remaining eleven were well on the way to Dusseldorf, including "A" for Able.

Conditions for flying were not good; there were two very active weather fronts encountered en route, and the aircraft had to fly through ice bearing cloud but those who were not forced back reached the target in the early stages of the raid. There was already evidence of the attack as the fires started by incendiaries lit up the area marked by the pathfinders. Through occasional breaks in the thick smoke which hung over the City, it was possible to see the streets and buildings in the glow of the fires. "A" for Able droned steadily over the target and guided by the Bomb Aimer, the bombs were released at 0140 hours on the 12th June.

Pilot Officer Boyce then altered course for the route home, and barely had he done so when the Halifax was caught in the brilliant blue beam of a master light from a searchlight battery; seconds later, the dozen or so slave searchlights of the battery, automatically joined the master and coned the aircraft within their beams. There was no escape from the light and for two or three minutes "A" for Able flew on, while the crew waited in anticipation of attack by a night fighter or anti-aircraft fire.

Disaster struck without warning, as an ack-ack shell suddenly exploded just below the nose of the aircraft. Its shrapnel wounded the navigator (F/O Black), the bomb aimer (F/O Buck), and my cousin Cyril who was the most severely injured, having been hit in the head. Meanwhile, Pilot Officer Boyce was having difficulty flying the aircraft as the port wing had been damaged by flak. The engine exploded and caught fire; then the crippled kite went into a dive, seemingly out of control. Boyce gave the order, "stand by to bail out," and then "bail out," but quickly countermanded the order by saying, "the kite is under control."

The aircraft had dropped over three miles out of the sky, and now there was a real danger the damaged wing would fall off giving the aircrew no chance to escape. Boyce gave his last order, "abandon aircraft." Time was at a premium as the Halifax was less than 2000 feet from the ground. The navigator (F/O Black) jumped out of the rear hatch to safety, followed by the two gunners (Sergeants Hall and Gray), and the flight engineer (Sergeant Stewart). The bomb aimer (F/O Buck) also jumped to safety from the front hatch, after unsuccessfully trying to push Cyril out before him. Cyril was adamant that he wanted to stay in the aircraft, possibly because his injury made him feel incapable of undertaking the parachute jump.

At 0200 hours on Saturday, 12th June 1943, "A" for Able ploughed into the German countryside, some thirty-four miles north-west of Dusseldorf, at a place called Uedemer Bruch. Presumably Cyril was on board, for he was initially buried in the local cemetery at Uedem which was close by.

Sergeants Gray and Stewart both seemed to recollect seeing the second pilot, Warrant Officer Tripp, bail out of the aircraft, but he was reported Killed in Action, and initially buried in Buderich Civil Cemetery, which is fourteen and a half miles east of where the aircraft crashed. It is possible his parachute failed to open, but there is no evidence to support this theory. Flying Officer Black, the navigator, reported that in his opinion the pilot had ample time to bail out and, although realising the danger, he would not leave the aircraft until all the crew were safe, so he stayed at the controls to give Cyril a chance of survival. The pilot (P/O Boyce) was initially buried in Monchen-Gladbach Town Cemetery, which lies thirty-four miles south of where the plane crashed.

The reason why P/O Boyce, W/O Tripp, and my cousin Cyril were initially buried in three separate cemeteries, miles apart from each other, will always remain a mystery.

The 1930s

My Cousin Cyril

I have little recollection of Cyril prior to 1929, which was the year I joined the choir at our local Church of St Luke in the Queen's Park area of Brighton. Cyril was also in the choir so we first used to meet each other at choir practice, the church service, tea parties and suchlike. At the age of seven, I did not go wandering far from our house, while Cyril lived a short distance away, and attended a different junior school, so it was not until three years later in 1932, when we were together in the Boy Scouts, and a year later attended the same senior school, the Brighton Intermediate, that our bond became firmly established. Cyril's full name was Douglas Edward Cyril Chambers, and he was born during July 1921, just ten months before me. We had the same great-grandfather, Edward Chambers (1834-82), so we were akin with the same family surname, and were more like brothers than cousins. I suppose the fact that he was always called "Cyril" was just one of those things, and it seems mere coincidence that my middle name is also "Cyril," but the affinity we had during the years before he was lost, was so great that it is not at all surprising. He had no siblings whereas I had an older brother, Vic and a sister, Wynne but strangely neither seemed so close to my heart as Cyril.

Much of our day-to-day spare time was spent in the company of mutual friends, both boys and girls, with the church and church hall the focal points for regular meetings. It was very much the anchor to which our lives were attached during the whole decade, and for nearly all that time the Rev. Oscar Brooks was at the helm. He made a big impression on both Cyril and myself, and indeed all the young people at the church. He had a terrific sense of humour and a flair for getting us to do anything for him. In return, we felt we had an adult friend who always had time for us and was great company. The organist and choirmaster was Herbert Elliott, who had been there so long he was almost part of the organ. He gave me my nickname of "Tuppenny" on my first day, by remarking that I looked like two penn'orth, meaning very small.

6

St Luke's Church c. 1938

Our church was dimly lit by gas, poorly heated by coke, and the organ bellows were pumped by hand. Trams trundled past the front porch. There was choir practice on Wednesday and Friday evenings, and two services with the choir on Sundays. Additionally, there were many special occasions, including weddings, which were popular because we were paid for attending. Of course, a reason for being in the choir was the fact we got paid, and pay night was quite an event. Herb Elliott kept an attendance register, and would make deductions from our pay for being absent. We would also be fined for misbehaviour; hence Cyril and I were each fined sixpence for talking behind the organ one Sunday, and there were undoubtedly many other similar reasons for being fined. Every choir practice would start with ten minutes of singing up and down various scales, followed by the forthcoming Sunday's music, and maybe an anthem or festival piece which was being rehearsed well in advance of its presentation. During the practice, we only used the choir stalls nearest to the organ, and had to turn and face Mr. Elliott. He was well acquainted with all the pranks and knew immediately, when I was flourishing a handkerchief with undue vigour one evening, that I was trying to dispense sneezing powder.

There was also an assistant organist, Mr. Bartley; we referred to him as "Uncle" Bartley. He was a well built man with a huge bushy moustache – a figure of fun for us youngsters and we played him up no end, but he was really very kind and also clever at his work of repairing clocks and watches at a shop not far from the church.

Cyril and I would always volunteer to take a turn at pumping the organ, which was quite a strenuous task. The bellows were hand operated by means of a large wooden beam, which protruded from the back of the organ, and had to be constantly moved up and down. Nearby was a narrow strip of glass let into the organ casing, behind which there was a white "mouse" suspended by a piece of cord. The "mouse" indicated how much air there was in the bellows; if it were at the bottom of the glass the bellows were full, and as the air ran out, the mouse would rise up the glass. It was necessary to follow the progress of the service, so as to anticipate when the organ was required, and for good measure the organist also signalled for air by pressing a button to illuminate a small torch bulb near the glass indicator. One Easter Sunday I recall pumping away throughout the rendering of Stainer's *Crucifixion*, and was not prepared when Herb Elliott trod on a pedal which activated all the organ stops, and every pipe wanted air to "*Fling wide the gates, Fling wide the gates for the Saviour waits to tread in his royal way.*" The "mouse" raced up the glass and I really had fears that the whole performance would fizzle out through lack of air.

A fleeting insignificant memory was a wooden post, which presumably supported the organ loft; it seemed to attract the boys who had pumped the organ, as initials were written or scratched on the woodwork over the years, so that it had began to resemble a totem pole, and we were no exception in adding ours.

The heating system was a coke-fired oven, which produced hot air that passed through ducts under the floor to gratings set into the aisles. On occasions when there was a procession around the Church, we went as slowly as we could over the gratings, so as to prolong the warmth of the hot air coming under our cassocks. The gas lighting was just sufficient to enable the hymn and prayer books to be read. During choir practice, the only lighting during the winter months came from two gas lamps in the centre of the choir stalls, and one lamp on the wall near the organ. The rest of the church was in total darkness as well as being cold, and I recall this presented rather an eerie scene while we rehearsed the music.

The social activities of the church community took place in the hall, which was just across the road. This was previously the church, so it was solidly built and had pillars inside which restricted the overall use of the floor area. Nevertheless, they were useful for dividing the stalls at Bazaars and Jumble Sales. The jumble sales would be like an Aladdin's cave – brass bedsteads to real wooden furniture; china figures to patterned chamber pots; fox boa's to top hats which usually smelt of moth balls. There were whist drives of twenty or more tables, also socials and dances, when French chalk was sprinkled on the floor to aid the footwork!

Ken in Boy Scout uniform

The youth organisations met in the hall, usually every week. Scout night was on Thursday, and it was fun dressing up in the uniform – a tricorn khaki hat, khaki shirt, red neckerchief with lanyard, short navy trousers, socks with green tape on the garters, a sheath knife and whistle attached to a leather belt, and lastly a five foot scout pole. Cyril and I were in the Pewit Patrol of the 2nd East Brighton Troop. We learnt to cook on a wood fire, tracking, first aid, fire fighting, tying knots, and a host of things which gained us a badge to sew on our sleeve. We sang songs while sitting around a "camp fire," in the hall. The fire was a fake, and consisted of a few logs nailed together, behind which there was some red crepe paper illuminated by an electric bulb. A large stage had been erected at one end of the hall, which was often used for amateur events, the Scouts being no exception, and we gave cabaret performances to raise funds. The Scout Master, whose name was Caffyn, was tough and during PT sessions, he used to stand in the centre of the hall and shout "Come on boys," and about twenty of us would rush to grapple him to the floor.

1934

An Idyllic Summer

This was the summer we first visited a small farm in Spithurst, a tiny village twelve miles from Brighton. Our treasured friendship with this farming family, Ernest (Erne) and Millie Carey came about when Cyril and I stayed at the farmhouse for a holiday, an arrangement made by my sister. The farmhouse faced a narrow country road with an orchard along one side, which adjoined the churchyard surrounding the village church. It was idyllic. They looked after us well, and we had a super time exploring the nearby fields and woods, also the upper reaches of the River Ouse which was a good walk away.

Cyril (right) and Ken with young Ray at Spithurst

We got on fine with their sons, Bernard, who helped
with the farming, and Ray, who was quite a young boy still
at junior school. Assisting Erne and Bernie to muck out the
cowshed and bring in the hay was part of the fun. They
showed us where to locate rabbits and how to set snares on
their runs; we learnt a lot about the country from them, and
we were sorry when it was time to go home.

1935

First Meeting of the Junior Detective League

The year 1935 was renowned for the Silver Jubilee of King George V, but it was also the year and month, in May, that Cyril and I got together, along with another boy Roland Joanes (Jonah), and decided to start a Club which we called the Junior Detective League; JDL for short. The three of us had met at my parents' house, and a minute book was started with the first meeting on the 25th May. Jonah, who was also a choir boy, was two years behind Cyril, and a year behind me at the same senior school, so our respective ages in 1935 were 14, 13 and 12. I cannot recall what prompted the formation of the JDL, or why it was so named as we did very little detecting. Perhaps, we had been reading too many comics? However, throughout the following four years other boys joined us, although there were never more than about half a dozen members at any one time, we all made some firm and true friends as a result. The minutes of the meetings, and a hand written "Gazette," contained in ten school exercise books, give a fascinating insight to our adolescent years. We held the meetings like grown ups and initially all took a turn at being the Chairman, Secretary and Treasurer.

One particular activity was camping. The holiday at Spithurst the year before had been unforgettable, and it was somehow arranged that the JDL went there to camp in August 1935. We begged or borrowed a tent and packed groundsheets, blankets, billy cans, tinned food, candles and matches. The complete logistics of this initial venture now escapes me, but I recall we had the time of our lives; it was real "Boy's Own" story book stuff. We sang the scouting songs while sat around a proper camp fire, and then, in the stillness of the night, listened to the chirping crickets, hoots of owls, and the cries of a vixen. Each day, we went into the woods to collect dead branches for the fire, often walking waist deep in the ferns, finding snakes and disturbing pheasants.

The JDL set up their campsite

One day we went to the river Ouse, passing a blacksmith's en-route and stopping while he shoed a horse. It took us nearly an hour to reach the Anchor, a small remote hotel situated by a weir on the river, the narrow road which only went as far as the building was no more than a cart track, and went astride a railway crossing which Cyril and I knew from our walk the previous year. The Anchor hired out flat bottomed boats which could be paddled upstream, for well over a mile to a waterfall, and this time we hired one. Learning only from practice, we manoeuvred the boat up the river, not always avoiding overhanging bushes and trees, which left leaves and twigs in the boat. We rested at times, watching cows drinking at the river bank, we wondered at the colourful dragonflies hovering above wild flowers at the water's edge.

Fish would jump up to catch flies, leaving a momentary ring on the water, and water-boatmen also left their mark; now and again we surprised a kingfisher or water vole when quietly paddling round a bend in the river. We came across a junction and went to the left as it was wider, but it turned out to be a dead end and we had to paddle back and take the right fork. There were small tributaries which could only be negotiated by lying nearly flat in the boat, but it was exciting, and as we went along one and through the bushes spotted a church. It was difficult to get out of the boat because of the dense vegetation surrounding the narrow stream, but we managed to scramble through a gap and crossed a field to investigate our find, which stood on its own, surrounded by fields with no other buildings in sight. The Church was open, so we went inside. An atmosphere of stillness took hold of us, and we spoke in whispers whilst almost tip-toeing around the interior, peering here and there. We found a chapel containing a number of tombs, and gazed in amazement at one which had the effigies of a knight in armour, his two wives, and their nine children who were all laid in a row according to their size; we were exploring and thus enthralled at our discovery. Later we were to find out that the church was St. Margaret's at Isfield, dating back to 1280, and the Knight was Sir John Shurley who died in 1631.

St Margaret of Antioch, Isfield

Returning to the boat and the main river, we found a rope barrier across the water with a notice "Private," in the centre. This was apparently meant to be the end of our journey upstream but we were able to get past the slight barrier, and continued for some distance, amidst a forest of trees, until we reached a waterfall - a man made structure of large concrete or stone steps, several yards wide, which towered above the boat. The water was gently running down the steps, and after securing the boat, we had no difficulty in clambering to the top where there was a large expanse of water, more like a lake. There was a snake swimming in the water with its head held high, and it gave us the creeps. Having satisfied our curiosity, we decided to call it a day. Going back towards the Anchor did not take so much time and effort, and on the straighter stretches of the river, we sometimes rested the paddles to let the boat slowly drift, or we would paddle like mad while singing that well known song from the film "Sanders of the River." On this occasion, our first river venture, we met another boat being paddled by a couple, much older than us, and ended up having a race. I cannot recall who won, but the photograph they took of us in our boat, and later sent to me, is inscribed, "Best of luck to the Oxford crew." We reached the boathouse, after passing under a railway bridge just around the first bend, and moored the boat with the confidence engendered by having spent six hours on the water.

The "Oxford Crew" Jonah, Ken and Cyril

Retracing our footsteps to the camp site took a good hour; it was located on the outskirts of a large wooded area in one of the fields which was not being cultivated so there were plenty of mole hills, thistles and scrub (small gorse bushes). The field was some way from the farmhouse and we had to pass the wind-pump which supplied their water. This was a metal tower built over a bore hole which supported a large fan activated by the wind that, in turn, operated the mechanism for pumping water into a galvanised tank. We obtained our water from here, and filled buckets to take along with us to the tent. Then the three of us renewed the fire, cooked something to eat and made cocoa, before ending another adventurous day sitting alongside the blazing logs.

We never tired of walking in the fields, woods and quiet roads in the area by day and by night; doing our own thing, sleeping when tired, eating when hungry. The weather was not always kind, there was rain at times and we found the tent leaked, but running a finger down the canvas from the point of the leak stopped most drips, and nothing stopped our enjoyment. There were to be many more times like this, which became better as we became older and wiser.

Cyril. Ken and Bernie (centre) at the farm.

When the camp came to an end, I guess we returned home somewhat tired but in high spirits due to the fact it had been such a success. However, another first in the JDL minute book was soon the subject of discussion, Guy Fawkes! It was agreed we purchase a few fireworks at a time, beginning two or three weeks beforehand. The 5th November was a Tuesday, but it made no difference, we met after tea and had a great time setting them off in one of our back gardens. When the show was over, we went to The Level, a recreation ground surrounded by elm trees in the centre of Brighton. The great attraction here was the bonfires, as a large number of people celebrated Guy Fawkes Night at The Level and the fires ranged from a large one in the centre, which had been built up over the preceding days with domestic waste including mattresses, to small wood fires surrounded by three or four people having their own party. The whole place was lit up with possibly thirty or more bonfires, and fireworks were going off in all directions. Our purpose was to join the throng standing around the main communal fire and simply watch it burn, while becoming smoked like kippers. Later in the evening the fire brigade arrived to extinguish what was left of the fires, then the next day Corporation workmen cleared up the debris, so except for burnt patches on the grass everything was back to normal. At the following JDL meeting it was declared a successful evening, but Cyril made a comment that he thought we had too many fireworks, and if there were less, we would have taken more care over them. I think this indicated that we lit several together, instead of one at a time.

Throughout November and early December we had been attending the vicarage twice a week for a course of instruction to prepare us for Confirmation. There were a number of us from St Luke's, and the Vicar made us comfortable in his lounge while he took us through the theology of the church, the services, and ensured that we knew the prayers. During the last session, we had to pass a test of sorts, which was not hard for me as I had already been in the choir and Sunday School for six years. Our Confirmation took place at St Luke's on December 12th 1935, when the candidates were required to approach the Bishop, two by two, for the laying on of hands. Cyril and I went forward together, dressed in our cassocks and surplices, and I have no doubt that Jonah was somewhere in the line up. After the service we were each given a special prayer book inscribed with our name, place and date of Confirmation, signed by the Vicar, and also the Lord Bishop of Lewes, Hugh Lewen, who had signed below the text "*Be thou faithful even unto death.*" Upon looking back, I think this was a stepping stone in the process of growing up and the fact we could now fully partake of the Eucharist, along with our elders, gave us a sense of belonging.

Interior of St Luke's Church

A week later, we commenced another annual activity, that of carol singing. It was not just a case of haphazardly going around the streets singing a carol in a doorway then knocking and asking for money. The choirboys were much more sophisticated. We first obtained a chitty from Herb Elliott, which certified we were members of St Luke's choir and as such were authorised to sing carols; armed with this, a group of us would proceed along a planned route which took in what we considered to be the most receptive or affluent residents. The streets were very dark, with few lights and no vehicles, so we took a hurricane oil lamp, supplemented with torches, to light our way and, if necessary, to view our carol sheets. Time was not wasted, we knocked first and then enquired of the occupiers whether they would like some members of the choir to render a few carols. The system worked well, for we rarely got turned down, and at the bigger houses were sometimes asked into the hallway, then after singing three or four carols we would be treated to ginger wine and cake. At this rate we were not able to make all that many calls in an evening, but after seven evenings each of us would have accumulated a worthwhile number of shillings.

1936

Home Life and the Slipper Baths

Shortly into the year 1936, the nation was mourning for our King, George V, who died on January 20th at 11.57. My Boy Scouts' diary does not mention whether it was am or pm, but everyone was very sober for days after; there were many laurel wreaths, black ribbon arm bands and Union Flags flying at half mast. The next day at the JDL's 28th meeting we had a discussion about our late King. I would imagine we came to the conclusion that in spite of the fuss it made little difference to our own lives. His funeral was held on Tuesday, January 28th, we had a day off school and there was two minutes' silence at 1.30pm. The Prince of Wales succeeded him as Edward VIII.

Cyril and I, accompanied by my mum, went to the Home Life Exhibition on the day before the King's funeral. This was not in Earls Court, London, but an offshoot version held in the Dome and Corn Exchange, here at Brighton. The two venues were linked together on these occasions; the Dome incorporated a large stage and a balcony, with seating on the ground floor which could be covered over, when necessary, for such use as exhibitions and dances. The Corn Exchange also had a sizeable floor area, and a small theatre. Together, the buildings provided an ideal space in which to erect the large number of exhibition stands required for the Home Life Exhibition. I particularly mention this because it was another popular annual event which we found entertaining, right up to the last one in 1939. We always managed to obtain plenty of free tickets and were able to make several visits over the weeks it was on, collecting loads of free samples and knick knacks, badges, stickers and so on. It was fascinating to watch demonstrations of supposedly new gadgets and hopefully to sample the end products while sales were taking place. On one occasion I recall watching a salesman make waffles in order to flog the waffle maker. This was merely a small square aluminium frame at the end of a piece of wire, the frame was first dipped in batter and then held on the surface of boiling fat, it cooked in no time, the batter came away from the frame and the result was a waffle. The demonstration sold the gadget by the dozen, while Cyril and I tucked into the waffles which had served their purpose - they were very tasty with honey! Periodically each day/evening there would be a band performance on the stage, usually accordions, mandolins or such like, which one could watch in comfort from the balcony, although the activity around the stands continued. Good entertainment and it was free!

The first JDL Annual Dinner took place on 22nd February at 8.30 pm. and looking back at the record it now seems like the Mad Hatter's tea party. It was held at my house, and we had some invited guests. The menu, written by Cyril, was:

Crème of
Tomate Soupe

Fillet of Huss et
Pommes de Terre

Fromage et Biscuits

Fruit

Crepes

The JDL dinner menu 1936

However, I can well remember that this turned out to be, Heinz tomato soup, fish and chips from a shop up the road, a packet of cream crackers and cheese portions, tinned pears and cream. Still, it was enjoyable, with speeches afterwards and the presentation of a gift to Mum for her help. This was another event destined to be repeated each year with increasing sophistication.

Cyril's time at school came to an end in July, and he commenced work in the office of the Co-op Dairy, which considerably curtailed his free time, except evenings and weekends. This brings to mind the play or operetta which the school performed in Cyril's last year. It was called *"Under the Castle Wall"* and was written by one of the masters. Cyril and I were in the cast. My role was that of a young villager, dressed as a girl, who joined others in a maypole dance, winding and unwinding the ribbons. At one of the evening performances, my nose started to bleed and I danced around with my head held back, literally in a bloody mess, until I was able get off the stage. However, Cyril had a speaking part as an older yokel and during one of the acts he told a story while the villagers were grouped around him. It started with the words *"Did I ever tell you the story of how I saved the mail? 'Twas one winter's eve, in June I believe, by gum, it's a gory tale."* I just wish my memory held the remainder of the story, for he carried it off so well.

Prior to Cyril starting work the JDL made regular visits to the Slipper Baths, visits which ceased altogether the following year when I moved to a modern house which had a bathroom. There was no such luxury in the Victorian terraced houses which made up most of the town and I recall we had a galvanised bath tub which hung on the wall in the backyard of our old house. Bath night would involve bringing the tub into the scullery, filling it with hot water from the copper, then sitting in it and washing all over with coal tar soap. I cannot say when that performance was overtaken by going to the slipper baths, but in the early days of the JDL we went together, usually on a Saturday morning, taking a towel and the fee of three pence to the premises, known as the Cobden Road Baths, which were conveniently at the end of Cyril's road.

Cobden Road Public Slipper Baths

It was an ornate red brick Victorian building fitted out with numbered cubicles in a long row each having a six foot bath. The water was controlled by an attendant who carried a handle to operate the valves that were situated outside the cubicles, and when allocated a vacant one he turned both the hot and cold water on while the occupant tested the bath for temperature before closing the door and getting undressed. Amusement was caused at this stage if it was discovered the water was then too hot or too cold as the procedure was to call out the cubicle number with a request for more cold or hot water, and the attendant would come and turn on the appropriate tap acting on shouted instructions from the occupant who was usually stark naked inside the cubicle. We would also converse with each other through the partitions and it was always an enjoyable occasion.

Fortunately, although Cyril was working on Saturday mornings, we now all had cycles which put the twelve miles to Spithurst in easy reach, and we hit upon the idea of 'hoboing', at least that is what we called it. During the warmer weather, we would pack enough food for three meals then ride over to Church Farm on a Saturday afternoon. Erne allowed us to sleep overnight in the barn; admitted we had the company of two cows in the stalls, an owl, and possibly some rats although we never saw any, but we were able to travel light without the camping gear and did not have to pitch a tent. There was a hay loft, accessible by a ladder, and we slept on the hay and used sacks as blankets. Below the loft was the usual farm gear, along with slabs of linseed oil cake, sacks of potatoes or such like, which made comfortable seating and a table for our eats. It was, of course, not possible to light a fire or even smoke in the barn, and our meals were simply sandwiches, cake and chocolate, with milk or water to drink. Thus we had the whole day on Sunday in which to enjoy our wonderful countryside before cycling home in the evening. While on some of these ventures, and also on our longer camps which included a Sunday, we were able to attend Spithurst Church at the 8am communion service, for we had now been confirmed. The Vicar had a white beard and seemed a benevolent elderly gentleman; he actually used proper bread for the host, which I have never since experienced. This was really in keeping with the small peaceful church, in the heart of the country, and the service added to our enjoyment of these times.

There was an evergreen "monkey tree" in the front garden of the farmhouse, so named because it is the only tree which cannot be climbed by a monkey. I am not sure whether that is true or false, but that is what Erne told Cyril and me one day when we were hoboing at the farm; how we came to be in the garden at that time, discussing the tree, I cannot recall. Nevertheless the episode is vivid in the mind because, after some banter, Erne promised us a pound if one of us could climb up the tree. This looked an easy way to get some money, so we each borrowed wellington boots, gloves and a hat, confident that these would protect us from the spiky green leaves which made up the branches. We then set about the task, only to find that neither of us could even get beyond the first branch although we both tried several times, there was no way of getting any hand or foothold on the branches, and we had to admit defeat. No doubt Erne knew his pound was safe!

The monkey tree outside the farmhouse

It was not that tree, but an oak in the woods, which was the cause of Cyril getting a scratched and bruised leg. He was limping as we walked to the farmyard and Erne asked what the trouble was. Upon being shown, in an instant he remarked: "I know what's good for that," then disappearing into the cowshed he came out with a large tin containing a pink jelly. "Cow ointment," he said, "It's good for everything," and slapped some on Cyril's leg. It apparently did the trick, and it was our first introduction to cow ointment, the cure for all external ills; smelling pleasantly of cloves, we were given some in a small container for our first aid kit!

Another day, when Cyril and I had mucked out the cow shed, Erne came along and together we leaned on the gate looking at the concrete area where the muck was piled prior to spreading in the fields. There a dry hard crust on the top, which we already knew to our cost, could not be stepped on without getting covered in cow dung up to the waist. Erne suddenly remarked "When I'm gone you can throw me in that lot." We had a good laugh at the thought. I am sure we looked upon farmers as a breed apart who, along with those who lived in the country, were all very much attached to their surroundings, the countryside and the animals, as well as being very friendly.

"*The JDL members then had the pleasure of seeing the Hindenburgh, and then went up to the Race Hill.*" Cyril entered this in the minutes of the meeting on Sunday, 5th July 1936. Our meetings were usually held after Sunday Evensong, and it is my guess we saw the airship at about 7.30, after a short club meeting, although regrettably I have no recollection of this event. It seems we failed to mention the Hindenburg's tragic end a year later. The club suffered the doldrums during the rest of 1936. Two new members had been taken on early in the year, but they did not take the meetings seriously enough so we stopped them coming. Nevertheless, by the year end we had successfully recruited another member, from the choir, Owen Gurton, who proved to be most helpful and became a staunch friend. Cyril compiled the minutes of the 34 meetings held throughout the year, and our club activities, along with the choir, Boy Scouts and other friends, went on as usual.

1937

Out to Work

1937 was quite an eventful year. The JDL dinner was held on 13th January with the usual hilarious menu. An Easter camp was planned but regrettably for some reason Cyril could not attend and another school friend of mine, John Bower, joined Jonah and me for the camp. This arrangement worked out very well for John's father, who owned a car, took us and our kit to Spithurst on Good Friday, 26th March. I recorded that we spent a nice night but it was cold and there was snow on the ground in the morning, nevertheless with the energy spent walking about during the day and the camp fire blazing at night we overcame the temperature and had a jolly fine time until John's dad came to pick us up on the following Tuesday. A couple of weeks after that my parents moved to a more modern house which was still in the vicinity of St Luke's Church and my friends, but it was not so large and the JDL lost their regular club room. We therefore continued to meet, more or less weekly, in one of our homes.

The highlight of the year was no doubt Coronation Day on the 12th May when the town was alive with festivity; there were flags, bunting and coloured lights everywhere – on the buildings, on trees, even on the trams and also strung across the roads. I met Cyril in the morning and we went to Preston Park to watch a 21 gun salute being fired, we then walked all along the seafront and main shopping thoroughfares admiring the decorations; together we listened to the King's speech and went to the seafront again in the evening to see a magnificent display of fireworks which were set off from the end of both the piers. It had been a full day of togetherness with Cyril and I finally arrived back home at 12.30 am So George VI had now been crowned, and surprisingly there was no mention in the JDL minutes or my diary of Edward's abdication during the previous year.

Shortly after the Coronation I left school and started work in the offices of Ronuk Ltd, a floor polish manufacturer, based at Portslade which was three to four miles along the coast towards Worthing. This came about because I had previously learned there was a job as an office 'boy' available there so I had written to the firm, obtained an interview and was then advised I could start on the 18th May. It was as simple as that, and I wrote to the school's headmaster explaining the position, which was quite in order as I was only a week away from my fifteenth birthday and in the final school year which would end in July. My birthday on the 26th was celebrated a day later, in the evening after attending the Scouts, when I entertained Cyril, Jonah and Owen to supper which consisted of soup, pies, spuds and salad.

Office hours at Ronuk were from 8.30am to 5pm and 12.30pm on Saturdays, but I was often much later leaving work, and as a point of interest the salary was twelve shillings and sixpence (12/6d) per week. My free time was similarly curtailed like Cyril's had become a year previously when he started working, but the JDL continued undaunted. On August 2nd, which was a Friday, choir practice night and pay parade, I received six shillings and then walked to the seafront with Cyril and Jonah to see the aircraft carrier "Courageous" and the destroyer "Crusader" which were moored off the Brighton beach. They looked a fine sight and attracted quite a crowd which gave the "Skylark" together with many other smaller fishing boats some extra business taking passengers out to sea for a closer look.

A weekend camp in September was followed by the first air raid trial for the town which took place in October. We had made no plans to meet up for this event and there was barely a mention of the fact in the minutes, but a newspaper cutting had been inserted from which I must quote a small extract as this was the start of things to come which would change our lives:

> "A trial air raid on Brighton....All the drama, horrors and realism of an attack from the air will be enacted in a special area in the Kemp Town district, the dates selected being the afternoon of Saturday 16th October and during the night of 23rd-24th October. RAF planes will make the raids:

smoke bombs and flares will be used.... The street lamps and public lighting will be extinguished and the public are invited to co-operate by putting their household lights out or screening them. The grim business of air raid precautions, fire fighting, rescue work, and first aid will be carried out, following the firing of a maroon."

I saw little of the Saturday afternoon rehearsal except the aircraft flying overhead but I deliberately went out during the night exercise at 11.00pm – it was pitch black and smoke bombs and flares added to the drama of the occasion – according to my diary I saw men in action, might have my photo in the papers and went to bed at 2.10am. My photo did not appear in the papers!

We seem to have forgotten Guy Fawkes on November 5th for there was no arrangement for us to meet up as in the past, in fact I went to the cinema in the evening with my girl friend of the day and saw the film Captain Courageous. Girl friends were beginning to take a part in our lives

The 100th JDL meeting was celebrated at Cyril's home on 19th December by a toast with wine; then during the four evenings prior to Christmas day we all went carol singing and shared the proceeds. I received fifteen shillings, three and a half pence – more than my week's pay at Ronuk.

1938

Off on a Cycling Holiday

"Little Red Riding Hood" was a very good pantomime and the show was part of the choir's outing on the 3rd January 1938; we all met at a café in the town for a slap up tea at 6pm then went on to the theatre at the end of the Palace Pier for the evening performance. It was quite eerie for us walking on the pier in the evening, at that time of the year, as it was only open for the theatre goers; the lights were dim and there was no activity such as that laid on in the summer months for the tourists. This theatre had around 1100 seats and was quite a popular venue all the year round, even though walking the length of the pier was not pleasant when the weather was wet, windy, and the sea rough. There was another theatre at the end of the West Pier with 450 seats, and the JDL often went to see the plays which were performed here; courtesy of Owen who provided free tickets obtained from his dad who got them for having a bill-board advertising the shows outside his hardware shop. We also obtained free cinema seats from the same source. I guess we were spoilt for choice with seventeen cinemas, five theatres, an ice stadium and the Dome Concert Hall.

The excitement of the choir outing was nothing compared to the prospect of acquiring a clubroom, which was in the air at this time. We had decided, several months back, to produce a JDL Gazette containing articles about our activity and circulate this among our elders in the hope it would lead to getting some place to meet. The Gazette turned out to be a school exercise book of 43 handwritten pages containing 18 articles relative to the JDL and produced by the members. I think it took me about four weeks to collect their scripts and re-write them, including my own, in the exercise book; it seemed all very serious at the time but reading the text now I find it very amusing and it is a shame I cannot reproduce more within this story, but perhaps an extract or two will raise a smile.

On Hobbies – *"As I sit here writing on this golden spring day I can see buds breaking on a tree in a nearby garden. The birds are singing on the house tops while within this room I see a bunch of primroses and a few daffodils.*

Looking out of the window once again I can see the grass green and fresh on the next door lawn. Oh how I would like to be out in the country on my bicycle! Cycling is perhaps the most beneficial exercise. Every present member of the JDL belongs to the Lukonian cycling club and on the run to Arundel, the first of the season incidentally, my bicycle took a fancy to falling to pieces."

On Camp – *"If it is wet we arrange the basins and pots under where the rain comes in, then find the driest spot in the tent and play cards until the rain stops."*

On Club Work – road signs *"Had there been a sign he might not have seen it or just glanced at it and then forgot about it, on the other hand if he had learnt them and acted accordingly he would certainly be better off still cycling than in a bath chair, hospital or even under the earth."*

In the event I believe only half a dozen persons read the Gazette, including the Vicar who enquired whether he could help in any way, but it was our own inspiration which solved the problem of our meeting place. Our activities at the church hall, mentioned earlier, lead us to come across a wooden hut on a secluded piece of church land behind the hall which at one time may have been used as a garden shed. The hut was about 8' x 6' and was near to the rear door, but also accessible through an iron gate set in the church surrounds. We learned it was in the possession of the Rangers (Senior Girl Guides) but it seemed to be in disuse so Cyril and I went to see the Vicar to speak to him on the matter after choir practice on the 7th January. He seemed nearly as enthusiastic as we were and promised to have a word with the Ranger's leader. Ten days later we went to the hall during the Guides evening and saw the leader (Miss Jones) who told us it was OK for us to have the hut, we were overjoyed and hastened to tell the others the good news. At long last we had a place to meet and its situation could not have been better.

We lost no time in starting to refurbish our Headquarters, for that is what we named it. I purchased a gallon of creosote for one shilling and three pence and we all set to on the following Saturday afternoon painting the woodwork, even the Vicar turned up to help. We obtained glass for the windows, linoleum for the floor, decorated the inside, made seats from wooden boxes or packing cases, and our first meeting was held there, after Evensong on Sunday

30th January 1938, by the light of a hurricane lantern which
Dad lent me. According to a note appended to the minutes
by Cyril, we met up a day or so after, in the evening, and
went around the shops to look for a lamp but did not
purchase one; on the way back I found, in the rejected coin
slot of a cigarette machine, a farthing which had been
carefully filed down to resemble the size of a sixpence;
evidently it didn't work and the specimen was kept for
inspection!

Queens Park Road. Brighton.

The church hall in Queens Park Road

Later we were given a Victorian table lamp with two
wicks and a tall glass globe which provided heat as well as
light, and there was much more done to make the HQ a
snug hideout over the coming months, such as retrieving a
table, over-mantel with a mirror, and an iron chest all from
the church jumble sale. We also fixed curtains over the door
and window to stop the draught. In January the JDL dinner
had been a great success; and there were also many visits to
the Home life Exhibition as Ronuk had a stall there and I
could get as many complimentary tickets as I wanted.

I went to the Vicarage on the 7th March and took my
air pistol and 100 pellets which the Vicar had asked me to
lend him. I've no idea why he wanted the gun, however it
was an opportunity to have a heart to heart chat with him
and he persuaded me to visit a dentist as my teeth were

giving me some trouble. Three days later a dentist, recommended by the matron at the Ronuk factory, extracted two teeth and the Vicar gave me five shillings towards the bill. Such was our great clergyman and friend whom we all respected, and I know Cyril in particular went for many walks with him on the surrounding Downs. My dental treatment eventually ended on 26th April, after another two extractions and several temporary fillings using gutta-percha followed by the permanent silvery mixture. I well remember the drill which was operated by a foot pedal like a sewing machine; a slow and painful experience. The total bill came to two pounds fifteen shillings.

Between times, on Friday, 25th March, I went to choir practice and the choirmaster, Herb Elliott, took me off the pay roll because I had reached the croaking age – a broken voice, so Sunday 27th was my last service as a choirboy. In celebration, during Evensong, the older boys in the choir stall where I ended my eight years as a soprano, consumed one shilling's worth of sweets and ate three marshmallow pies with a little wooden spoon; I hasten to say in the dim gaslight. I should imagine that both Cyril and Owen would have preceded me by a year; however none of us ended our presence in the stalls, including Jonah, as we were all altar servers and were also soon back again in the choir with a different voice.

The JDL 1938. Left to right (front) Ken's brother Vic and Jonah (back) Owen, Ken and Cyril.

Another camp took place at Easter 15th to 18th April. Jonah was away, and with our various commitments the arrangements for the rest of us getting to the camp were quite complicated, but we all made it and had a great time.

My old school friend John Bower was now living and working at Church Farm since being introduced to Erne at last year's Easter Camp, but his father transported our kit together with John's older brother Steve, who started to join in. We were soon back again camping over the Whitsun holiday 4th to 6th June, which came soon after my birthday (26th May) when all the lads came to my house for a slap up tea, JDL style. Three weeks after Whitsun I set off with my elder brother, Vic, on his tandem for a two week tour to Yorkshire stopping overnights at Youth Hostels. We intended to visit my father's old 1914/18 wartime comrade, who lived near Dewsbury.

My brother had become involved with the JDL; he came camping with us a few times and there was an occasion when Cyril rode on the back of the tandem when his own cycle was out of action. He was three and a half years older than me and had bought the tandem mainly to go cycling together with his girl friend, so I cannot recall how the idea of touring with him to Yorkshire came about. Nevertheless we became members of the Youth Hostel Association and arranged to coincide two weeks of our holidays, then meticulously planned the route to various Hostels avoiding the use of major roads as much as possible.

We set off on Saturday, 25th June 1938 with my brother at the controls while I sat behind holding the fixed handle bars; our kit was packed in panniers either side of the back wheel. After our first overnight stop at Bucklebury in Berkshire we headed for the hostel at Stoneleigh in Warwickshire, only to be told it was closed so we had to race another thirty miles to Lichfield. The weather had not favoured us and at the start of the third day we again needed our capes and leggings as we made our way through Stoke on Trent, Leek, and into the Peak District some 1000ft up to Hartington. We met two locals while pushing the bike uphill and they spoke about the area, mentioning Thors Cave where the sun is supposed to set on the entrance on the longest day of the year, a tale originated by the Druids, and also of Iram where the river flows underground; then with their good wishes we carried on to the hostel, Hartington Hall. This was the second largest in the country with accommodation for 118, but there were only seven of us members and a party of school children staying that night. The Hall was, and probably still is, a fine place, built about 1640 with original oak panels in the dining rooms, also very large fireplaces – annex bedrooms and drying rooms etc., and we had a game of golf on the lawn outside, putting ten holes. There was also a good canteen and we were able to buy milk shakes. It was very wet and stormy during the night and after a breakfast of post toasties, egg and bacon we resumed our journey. This day, Tuesday, 28th June 1938, was the most dramatic for scenery and terrain so I have taken the whole entry from the log which I wrote during the evening at each hostel.

"Started riding at 10.15. Weather: Cloudy & cold – pullovers on and capes & leggings 11.00-6.30. Rode and often pushing – passed a big lime works – down a very steep hill (dangerous to cyclists) to Millers Dale, terrific sloping sides. Heard blasting operations and saw a few blasts although not very big. On to Eyam, and after a stiff climb cycled down to Grindleford Bridge. Went into house (shop) and had ham & eggs, cakes and tea 1/11d. Very steep hill up but managed and then down six miles to Sheffield – a very big place, blacker than Stoke, many more coal mines and factories etc. Walls that were once red are now black with soot in the heart of the city – churches black – graves neglected – everything seems down and out and yet the factories humming and bustling, some nearly falling down. We passed coal mines on the way with huge slag heaps bigger than one could describe. A person not seeing the actual views could never imagine the immense slag heaps, the vast gorges of the Peak District, the old Roman lead mines, and how emotional the inhabitants are about their country. At Tickhill we turned left for the Rossington Hostel, crossing the Great North Road at Rossington where we watched a blue streamline express train pass at a level crossing. Found the hostel, Mayfields Farm, a very good place. Had tea of peaches & cream, cakes, bread & butter, tea. Wind, rain and clouds got our spirits down a bit as under such weather conditions cycling is not a holiday!"

It was a shorter ride the next day to reach our destination of Whitley, near Dewsbury and we arrived at 3.30 to be greeted by our father's wartime comrade Charlie Micklethwaite his wife Vi and their family, Doreen, Elsie and Laurie The cyclometer was not working properly but so far we reckoned to have travelled a good three hundred miles. I took the opportunity to write letters to home, Cyril, and a girl friend.

Our hosts looked after us very well with real Yorkshire fare; we had a good night and during the following day Charlie took us down the coal mine where he worked in some managerial capacity. The mine, which did not have a shaft but went into the side of a hill, was only a few fields distant from his cottage so we walked to the entrance and after being equipped with safety lamps we entered into the dark whilst sitting on a truck running on rails. Charlie explained the workings, coal seams etc. and we went about half a mile bending low all the time. We passed one junction where we took the lower passage, but as the coal face was nearly two miles down track we did not go further, which was just as well for it was necessary to put the lamps on the truck and push it back up the rails to the entrance, nevertheless it was a interesting experience and we ended a restful day by visiting Whitley Church.

Friday, 1st July, we said goodbye to our hosts and headed for our next port of call, the hostel at Bempton which was a couple of miles north of Bridlington and within sight of the Flamborough Lighthouse. When reaching Leeds it became necessary to don our rain gear, and while at York we encountered a thunderstorm and had a spill in the Shambles of all places! The back wheel slid and I came off the bike fortunately with no damage except my static handle bars were slightly bent. There was some concern that the two May 1937 Coronation mugs, packed in our panniers, might be broken; these were inscribed "*Whitley Villagers Welfare Society*" and had been presented to us as a memento of our visit, although it was a year later. We found them intact when we arrived through pouring rain at Bempton hostel, having completed the eighty mile stretch from Whitley and reaching the northern limit of our itinerary.

The worst weather was encountered the next day starting with a thunderstorm on our approach to Hull via Hornsea, however this cleared at Hull and the ferry crossing

(11d each) to New Holland was calm. We had a further twenty-five miles to cycle before reaching the hostel at Glentham, a village some twelve miles north of Lincoln, and slightly east of Caenby Corner which is on the A15 a straight Roman road (Ermine Street), but we were keeping to parallel byways and were within a couple of miles when the heavens opened with torrential rain, brilliant flashes of lightning followed by startling claps of thunder. There was nothing we could do but press on and after ten minutes it was replaced by light rain until we reached the hostel. Fortunately it was one of the best for food - chicken and salad for supper; then we pondered over the rest of our route which would have taken us into Suffolk, Essex and Kent via the Tilbury-Gravesend ferry. The weather had given us second thoughts about carrying on for another five days and it was decided to cut the programme short then head for home with just one more overnight stop at the Houghton Mill hostel near Huntingdon.

After a satisfying breakfast of porridge followed by three rashers, an egg, a sausage and fried bread, we set off refreshed and in better weather. Following a more direct route we covered the eighty or so miles in a reasonable time and found we had made a good choice of hostel accommodation for our last night. The warden lived separately from the hostel which turned out to be an old watermill actually built on the River Ouse, with the original machinery lying about rusty and dirty. The whole place except the foundations was built of wood and we thought it a most interesting building and location. We did not have any meals here so presumably we were directed to a café or such. The next morning, Monday, 4th July 1938, were on the road at 8.15, which was earlier than usual for we had a long way to travel; taking the main road to Royston then following the A10 through Ware and Tottenham. It took us one and a half hours to cycle six miles through London, crossing the Thames by London Bridge and getting on to the Brighton road but after that it was plain sailing, with a stop at Sam's Halfway Café we reached Brighton and were back home at 7.30pm having cycled 125 miles on the last day which brought the overall total to over 700 miles.

I learned a great deal from this tour not only about the country but also about my brother who seemed very reserved compared to my usual friends. Perhaps it was the

3½ years age difference but I was never really at ease in his company; we did not have the same camaraderie as that which existed between Cyril and me. I could never understand why.

After the cycling adventure with my brother I had a few more days of holiday before returning to work at Ronuk, but I couldn't wait to return for I was very attracted to one of the girls, Doris Cooper who also worked there. Like me, she had a bike so we used to meet up and go cycling over the Downs on the outskirts of the town. It was just a brief encounter, lasting a few months, and is mentioned because that was a time, when we were sixteen or seventeen, that girls started to take a greater part in our lives.

The weather was set fair and the JDL started planning a camp for the bank holiday weekend at the end of July 1938. I was fitted for a gas mask (medium size) on Monday the 25th, a sign that war was on the horizon; then I met Cyril and we went to the JDL hut to fix a blind at the window, a blackout perhaps. There was a club meeting on the following evening, and we were all together again on Thursday evening at a meeting of the Church Communicants' Guild. I met Cyril again after work on Friday to go shopping for a tent and we eventually bought one for 7/10½. I am not sure why we wanted another tent, but we needed one for the stores and there was an increase in our number, especially if we could all arrange to get together at the same time. Saturday was a busy day, I left work at 12.35pm caught the train home, had a bite to eat before taking my kit to Steve Bower's who was going by car. I then called on Owen and we set off on our bikes, and were passed on the road by Steve with his dad driving the car. Arriving at Spithurst, Owen and I caught up with Steve, and also Jonah who had cycled earlier, and we all set to, erecting the tents and foraged for wood to make a fire. Cyril joined us at 10.30pm when we had supper and a chat around the fire before retiring about midnight. This is how Cyril described the occasion in the minute book:

> *"The JDL Camp was held in the usual place and consisted of five tents which were all pitched in the Second Grubs (this is a reference to the particular field at Church Farm). All members were present by Saturday evening and a supper*

of cream cheeses, biscuits and coffee was partaken by the entire company; it was an excellent evening and nobody was in any great hurry to retire. Owen and Jonah occupied the bell tent, Ken and Cyril used the ridge tent, and Steve slept in the hike tent. Being a warm evening, no one complained of the cold during the night, in fact all agreed that it was an excellent night's rest. Nevertheless, comfortable as it was, everyone managed to get up by 8.30 when the sun was already shining, a good beginning to an enjoyable day. The party with their washing kit left for the farmhouse or rather the cowsheds, for a primitive wash; refreshed by the cool water we returned to the site, by now it was becoming very hot and our apparel consisted only of slippers and shorts. A fire was made, the kettle put on and a breakfast of eggs, rashers and fried bread was prepared. After breakfast it was agreed to make a trip to the river for a bathe and on arrival at the Anchor Hotel by the river, we visited the tuck shop and consumed a plentiful supply of lemonade or orangeade according to taste. Following the river up in the direction of Isfield Church, a likely spot was found for swimming but this was unsatisfactory owing to weeds and an awkward passage to the water from the bank. Jonah and Steve nevertheless had an enjoyable swim, and then after Ken and Steve had finished climbing trees and Jonah had enough of swimming we retraced our steps back towards the Anchor Hotel. But before we arrived there, a magnificent place was found for us to resume bathing, a railway bridge, carrying the rails between Lewes and Tonbridge crossed the river, the girders of which made excellent diving boards. The water was free of weeds and everyone, including Ken who borrowed Cyril's costume, enjoyed a bathe while Jonah and Steve were not satisfied until they had jumped into the water from the top of the bridge. It was not until we were tired of swimming that anyone gave thought to the time, which we found to be gone 3.00pm; the tuck shop was again

patronized as we left with everyone buying to his
particular wealth, and we reached the farm about
4.30pm.

   We filled our water buckets, which had
been brought over from the camp earlier in the
day and walked the last lap of our journey across
the fields. Before dinner, a fire had to be made,
potatoes scraped and boiled, but by 6.00
everyone had finished eating and seemed pretty
tired; the heat was still terrific and the campers
were taking on the appearance of lobsters. Seven
o'clock found us ready for an evening's fishing
and a walk. The party, with fishing tackle, left for
Jordan's Pond situated between Barcombe Cross
and Spithurst; Steve had furnished everyone with
a line and bait so that each had an equal part in
the evening's entertainment, but one cannot tell a
fishing story in this account because no one
caught anything; anyway it was an experience for
some of us and was enjoyable. There was just
time for us to go down to the local pub for our club
and camp drink, cider, which we bought, to wit,
two flagons of the best and these were not
consumed until our arrival at the camp which was
about 10.00pm. It was now getting much cooler in
fact cold, all was still and quiet except for our
voices, all was dark around us enclosing us in a
kind of world of our own. Outside the moving
circle of light given from the smoking fire, which
completely surrounded the campers, all was dark
and still. We started to sing, old songs, new songs
and make a noise generally, then after we had
sung for an hour or more we got ready to retire for
the night; now and again somebody would stir the
fire when it showed signs of going out. The
embers were still burning when we left the
campfire for bed, but this did not mean sleep for
all of us; Steve in the hike tent still created a
noise, Ken and Cyril were still laughing and
jabbering, not a sound was heard from the inmate
of the bell tent, Jonah who was evidently fast
asleep, while Owen in the hospital tent was also
quiet."

The Anchor Hotel

I lived every word of Cyril's narrative in my memory of that day, and have a note giving the temperature as being 84° so there was little wonder we went to the river again the next morning, Monday, 1ˢᵗ August, to swim about under the bridge. We were unable to stay for long as my parents were coming to the camp in the afternoon and we had arranged to meet them, which we did at Barcombe station. The time passed quickly, with the preparation and consumption of dinner and tea, a game of cricket in the field and a walk in the woods. Cyril took a photo of me and my parents, he used an old box camera which we carried around at times; this was loaded with 120 roll film, sufficient for eight postcard size exposures and one never knew how they would turn out. All photographs of our activities were taken in that way and there were many poor results due to bad light or a shaky hand. We had to strike camp in the early evening and tidy the site. My parents returned by the 9.10 train; Steve was picked up by his father who came over in his car, he also took our kit back, except the bell tent which we left on site ready for an early return; the rest of us got on our bikes!

*Ken's parents
pay a visit to
the campsite*

Two weekends later, Steve and I cycled to Spithurst for
an overnight stay in the bell tent, we sat by a campfire in
the still of the night before retiring, then spent the next day,
between cooking meals, wandering in the woods and around
the fields before returning home. Another two weeks passed
and Steve and I were there again, along with Cyril and my
brother. As usual we cycled on the Saturday at different
times; Cyril and I went together arriving at 10.00pm. The
following day it was decided to walk to Piltdown pond
roughly three miles away, we had done this many times and
it was a nice stroll down a country lane. However, while
walking back we came across a very old cottage alongside
the road, which had not previously caught our attention; it
looked empty and inviting so we tried the door more forcibly
than we should have done and proceeded to investigate the
interior. I don't think we had managed to get upstairs before
there was a loud shout from the doorway and an irate man

was demanding to know what we were doing on the property, and as we walked out he wrote down our names and addresses. We continued on to the camp feeling very subdued and foolish but we heard nothing further about the incident; the picture shown was taken later and affixed to the JDL minute book - note the old bucket well on the right!

The old house that looked empty

On the 10th September I wrote in my diary *"Another Hitler crisis about Czech war."* Judging by the notes in my diary it seemed that war could well have commenced in September 1938, for by the end of the month trenches were being dug everywhere and gas masks were being issued. After arriving home from work on the 26th we started digging up the lawn to construct an air raid shelter, an area approximately 5' x 6'6" and the idea was to dig the chalk out to a depth of five feet, build walls to the height of six foot around the hole while making provision on one side for an entrance down some steps, the roof was to be made of timber beams covered with corrugated iron sheets with the chalk piled on top.

Working by the light of a storm lantern we dug down a foot of chalk; the following night we excavated another foot, then the JDL came to our aid on the next night the 28th, by which time the hole was four foot deep. I was also issued with a gas mask on this day. All around there seemed to be a sense of urgency but tension was somewhat lessened when we heard the Powers were meeting tomorrow. At the end of the month I noted that a peace plan had been agreed upon by the Four Powers and the sense of urgency suddenly disappeared although the preparations for war still went ahead. Thus work on our own shelter was continued with materials supplied through the Government and with much assistance at varying times by the JDL.

Ken trying the gas mask while working on ARP shelter.

The season had now changed with darker evenings and a cooler temperature. I enrolled for evening school the same as I had the previous year, a commercial course which took two hours twice a week; it seemed the thing to do especially as the study was at my old school. The JDL, along with others connected with St Luke's, were all doing their own thing yet often met up in the evenings and at weekends. Most of us had joined the Badminton Club which was started at the church Hall; the high net was strung between two of the pillars, while the court was marked out on the wooden blocks of the floor; I guess it was the correct size and anyway we had lots of fun hitting the shuttlecock back and forth, usually on a Saturday afternoon. Of course, any activity in the hall was handy for us as our hut was only a few paces away.

Owen and I, along with another friend, Richard Whittington (Dick), cycled to Spithurst early on Sunday morning, 1st October, then having picked some mushrooms we started back and on the way it poured with rain, soaking us to the skin; nevertheless in the evening we attended the church service. Dick, who was also in the choir, had a job in London with the Customs and Excise but he had shown much interest in our activities, evenings and weekends, thus he came to a JDL meeting on the 16th and was enrolled as a member. We cycled to Spithurst again on the Sunday 23rd; Cyril came with us this time and we walked across the fields to the camp site, only to find that the bell tent which had been left there had blown down and was flat on the grass. I was glad there were four of us as we were able to pack it up and carry it back to the farm, where we stored it in a disused pigsty. There were also some items of equipment missing, an axe, a groundsheet, a lamp, enamel ware and cutlery, and even a small tent was missing but it was our own fault for not clearing the site and leaving it for so long; no doubt being over confident by its remoteness.

There was a confirmation service at the Church on Tuesday evening, 1st November, which I attended with Cyril and Owen, when the latter was confirmed. Firework night passed without any interest for getting together this year; maybe we were becoming too old, for I landed up at a cinema to see the film "*King Kong*" by myself which was most unusual. It was a dismal time of the year, becoming dark early when the air was often very still and filled with smoke laden fog which descended in the evening; the result of smoking chimneys from hundreds of terraced houses in the town. However, work on the personal ARP shelter in the back garden had never let up and after a meeting on the 20th November we went to my parent's house where Cyril, Jonah, Owen and Dick were able to inspect the completed shelter they had all helped to construct.

At a JDL meeting some four weeks later we were making final arrangements for the JDL party which was to be held on the 27th; this was also a holiday as Christmas Day fell on a Sunday. For the first time we were going to invite girls and there was some discussion as to who these should be, then eventually invitations were sent out and accepted. Strange to mention, there is no record of their names - which now seems a dreadful oversight.

1939

The Early Months

Tennis, Girls and a Gloster Gladiator

An account of the Christmas party was given at a sort of AGM held on the 4th January 1939. *"It was agreed the Party was excellent, the girls that attended thoroughly enjoyed themselves and made the evening much brighter for all the members, including Frank Gander, the pianist, who joined in the fun. Tea was taken at 5.00, and at 6.15 everyone adjourned to the Drawing Room; a quiet game of "Guessing the advertisements" took place, and halfway through the evening there was an interval for port wine and biscuits while Frank played enchanting melodies on the piano; he also played several songs which were sung by all the guests. Postman's Knock took up most of the second part of the evening and even after an informal supper – some of the guests continued to play until 11.40 when the Party drew to a close. The usual presentation was made during supper by Cyril to our host, Mrs M.F. Chambers, for letting us hold the Party and the extra work it caused."* Arrangements were also made at this meeting for the members to meet at Cobden Road Baths at 6.50pm on Monday, 9th January, from where we would walk to the Palace Pier to join the St Luke's choirboys and visit the pantomime *"Mother Hubbard"* which was performing in the theatre at the end of the Pier. It turned out to be a good show and afterwards we walked back home with our Vicar, the Rev. O. E. Brooks.

Later in the month we all went to the Home Life Exhibition which was destined to be the last one. Cyril admirably described the occasion: *"An enjoyable evening was had by the JDL members at the exhibition on Friday last, 20th January, held at the Dome and Corn Exchange. After visiting the various stands, we made for the balcony to hear and see perhaps the biggest attraction, Alfredo's Gypsy Band. They were indeed good and they played a varied selection of music which we all thoroughly enjoyed. Unfortunately we did not see a great deal of the stands, at least we did not examine them very closely. We did not, as in previous years, see the films which the Brighton & Hove Gas Co. offered free of charge. The majority of time was spent*

*at the stand where "Astare" the "Miracle Mind" was
demonstrating, but despite suggestions no member could find
a flaw or clue as to how he managed to fool us. It was agreed
that there was some catch in the demonstration; nevertheless
it proved the biggest attraction of the stands. On the more
practical side, the Lullingstone Castle Silk Worm Farm was
interesting. Their stand covered the whole process from the
hatching of the silk worms to the reeling of the raw silk by
machinery. "Beauty bars" for ladies were a new attraction
this year and they seemed to be doing quite well; evidently a
great number of women think they need such treatment. After
a glass of Coco Cola and Toneca, better known as bottled
dynamite, we again listened to the band, the soloists being
Rex Rodger (Irish tenor) and Jack Mitchell (accordionist). This
ended our tour of the exhibition and we left the Dome at 10
o'clock."*

The complimentary tickets came from Ronuk who had
a stand there.

In the role of Outdoor Activities Manager, Cyril also
penned this amusing report on 27th January: *"The Cinema
De Luxe was honoured with our presence on the eventful
evening when the JDL en bloc went to see "The Adventures of
Robin Hood" which we all thoroughly enjoyed. The supporting
programme, though of a serious nature, caused much
amusement to us. With careful manoeuvring we left the
ninepenny seats for the shilling seats, but they were not
much better as the springs had long gone out of them also."*

There was excitement on 11th February when an RAF
plane crashed into a house very near to where we lived. In
seconds the plane and house were a raging inferno caused
by fuel from the burst tanks; the pilot along with three
people in the property died at the scene. It was misty at the
time and it was thought he had flown low to ascertain his
position and misjudged the distance. The type of aircraft
was not reported but from the burnt out tail plane it looked
to me like none other than a Gloster Gladiator. Thousands
of people were on the streets of Brighton on Friday, 17th
February to see the funeral cortege of the three victims, a
mother and her two children and it was estimated a further
five thousand had assembled in the cemetery to be present
at the committal; the pilot was buried later at Wallington
which was presumably his home town. The JDL met on the
following Sunday when the tragedy was discussed in sober

terms, little realising it would become insignificant within a short while. Then after having decided there would be enough seating accommodation for seven members, we also agreed that Steve Bower should join the Club provided he did not smoke his pipe in the hut.

On the last day of February I was sent home from work by the matron, who declared my high temperature made me unfit and I did feel rotten. The works' matron, Miss Napper, was an authoritative figure in her own domain, the sick room; it was here she attended to anyone who was not up to the mark. At her morning surgery she would dispense hot Owbridges or cold quinine for coughs and colds as if it was a wine bar. She treated cuts, sprains, bruises and boils and was deemed to be indispensable to the factory girls and office workers alike. I went to her on one occasion with a swollen hand caused by a horsefly bite, and she applied a poultice and a bandage. The swelling soon disappeared but the treatment was maintained for several days after which she inspected the hand closely and remarked, "It's strange I cannot see where the horse bit you!" Before I left the firm she had retired and was presented with a rocking chair which I thought was very suitable.

My sickness which was deemed to be the 'flu and kept me at home for nearly two weeks. The doctor called twice, as did the vicar who brought some novels; Cyril, Jonah, Owen and Dick were also visitors on some evenings when we played cards or board games. Lastly, I had the attention of two girl friends, Joan and Peggy, the latter bringing flowers, violets and forget-me-nots; it was fortunate the girls did not call at the same time! I was back at work on the 13th March and everything soon returned to normal, my time outside of work being taken up with meeting the boys in the hut or about the town, playing badminton in the church hall, attending the services and events, evening school and of course dating girls! A note in the diary on the 18th reminded me that the international situation was pretty grim again, but we seemed to be getting used to the threat of war, although much work was still in progress with air raid precautions; trenches had been dug on The Level, also in the parks and school playgrounds.

At the end of the month the JDL were busy arranging an Easter Camp which took place between 8th and 10th April, unfortunately Cyril could not get the time off work and

Owen cycled over for only one day but the rest of us had four good nights under canvas, spent some time on the river and had a midnight hike in spite of it being a bit cool at that time the year. My parents went away over the following weekend and the four stalwarts, Cyril, Dick, Jonah and Owen came to the house on the Saturday evening and we played Pontoon and Happy Families. Cyril stopped behind, when the others left at an hour before midnight, and we stayed up talking for a further two hours before retiring – it was one of those great times together and the night when the clocks advanced, so Summer Time had begun and we made up the hour by not surfacing for breakfast until 11 o'clock on Sunday morning.

Trenches being dug at The Level, Brighton in preparation for war.

The commencement of May brought tennis fever in place of badminton. One of the girls, Phyl Brook, had obtained the use of a grass court at a secluded spot close to the race course and alongside the Bear Road Reservoir which overlooked the town, so we moved our activity there for the summer. There was Phyl's sister, Bet, also Peggy, Muriel, Vera, Stella, Nancy and Hilda, are names which come to mind, while the JDL members comprised most of the male half of the tennis club. The girls were all great fun as well as being attractive and it was inevitable we boys would take a fancy to one, more than the others, thus there was some pairing as it was nice to have a special girl friend to go out with apart from playing tennis; they had now become part of our lives.

We had decided to invite the Vicar and the Curate to a JDL meeting which was our 144th and this was arranged for Tuesday, 23rd May when we all met in the hut at 8pm. My brother was the only one absent due to work; even so it must have been a squeeze to get all of us seated but it was a good meeting which lasted an hour, during which time we talked about our activities and the church. Our guests seemed genuinely pleased and it was nice to have the interest of adults.

On Whit Monday the 29th May it was my brother's wedding day when he married his girlfriend, Winifred, at St. Matthew's Church in Sutherland Road, Brighton. The choice of the church was a matter of parish boundaries as both our house and that of his girlfriend's parents were in the parish of St. Matthew. All the JDL members attended the service in the afternoon and afterwards, in the church hall for the reception when Cyril gave a speech full of humour about the JDL which was well received. The reception ended at 6.30 and I have no recollection of where the couple went to after we had dispersed; perhaps they rode away on the tandem – a bicycle made for two? My sister was 13 years older than me, she had married in August 1933, a year when Cyril and I were just young Scouts, and I do not recall her wedding with any clarity as I was a youngster and did not pay much attention to these family events. Nevertheless both my brother and sister-in-law were assets later on in my life.

A fine week's holiday was a good start for June, I spent much time on the beach with a friend, Monty Tyler, and the two girls Phyl and Bet; we made up a foursome for a short while. Monty lived near and attended the Church, he was a popular member of the tennis club and other activities. Then I went on Ronuk's annual outing for the staff, involving a coach trip to Richmond where we visited the Palace at Hampton Court together with its famous maze, and I first tasted "Maids of Honour" a type of cake which we ate at tea time. There were 21 girls and just two boys in our party under the eagle eye of the Matron, Miss Napper.

The very next day, Friday 16th, there was a reminder of war by another trial run for the ARP organisation when the whole of Brighton was blacked out, and incidents were designed to test all the services and communications. An odd chink of light shining through a window brought a knock on the door with a request to "put that light out." Motorists were asked to drive through the dark streets with sidelights only. Traffic lights were masked so that a cross appeared instead of a complete circle; traffic islands and other obstructions were marked with hurricane lamps showing a red light. There were two mock air raids by planes from Tangmere and during the first it was presumed the Town Hall had received a direct hit and caused casualties. There was another blackout exercise on Saturday, 8th July and we were certainly becoming more familiar with the situation. My father's army pal, Charlie whom Vic and I visited on the tandem tour the previous year, came with his family to stay with us for the last week in July. His eldest daughter,Doreen was the same age as me so, after work, I spent some time with her and showed her around the town. At work I was asked to take over the bulk of the gatekeeper's job while he went on holiday; this involved seeing that the factory girls clocked in and out, sounding the hooter for start of work at 8am and lunch time 12.30–1.30 and finish at 5.45. The hooter was also used as an ARP siren and would be sounded (wavering) for three minutes upon receiving a red alert and two minutes when getting the white all clear message. Additionally, there were visitors to direct and goods to receive; it made a change from the routine office work and I rather enjoyed myself.

Another camp for August Bank Holiday was arranged but it was difficult to get everyone together for the whole weekend, and when I cycled to Spithurst on Saturday afternoon 5th August it was to meet up with only Jonah and another companion, Basil Wooldridge. Nevertheless on the Monday we packed up the site early and left to meet the other JDL members, also Phyl and Bet. My bike had broken down so I did a lot of walking, but with much ingenuity nine of us managed to get to the Anchor Hotel at 2 o'clock where we hired a punt and had a great time on the river. Many hours must have been spent larking about on the river in the punt, for after leaving the Anchor Hotel we did not get back to Lewes railway station until the evening, when for some reason Phyl, Cyril, and myself decided to walk the further eight miles to Brighton while the other six caught a train; it was an odd choice to make, regretfully not recorded, but does not surprise me for we were in high spirits and after all it was a Bank Holiday. We probably took to the highway rather than the meandering footpath across the Downs, there would be very little traffic on the road and the moon at its first quarter would not have been bright. No doubt we chatted while walking as there was always a topic of conversation; one thing for certain – we arrived home at midnight – and this was one of those times which highlighted the strength of our companionship.

I was concerned about my bike which was at the Farm and required a new spindle for the back wheel, but as luck would have it I bumped into a friend, Jack Baker, two days later; it was late in the evening when I was returning home from playing cards in the hut, Jack possessed a motorcycle and in no time had agreed to take me to Spithurst on Saturday afternoon - luck indeed! I bought a new spindle from Halfords on Thursday evening (10th August 1939) when there was yet another and so far the biggest air raid exercise involving a blackout over all the south of England between 10.30pm and 4.00am No longer did these events provide me with any excitement and I preferred to go to bed. As arranged earlier, Jack Baker duly took me to the Farm on the back of his motor bike and helped replace the spindle then left me to pedal back. I noted the return journey took me one hour and twenty five minutes to travel just the twelve miles, my old Raleigh was falling out of favour by being too heavy, nevertheless it got me around.

Within a matter of days Cyril and I were again talking about holidays and the possibility of camping before the summer expired, and we had this in mind while continuing the activities of tennis, beach parties, the church, and trysts with girl friends. Strange perhaps to mention, but the latter was never once discussed among the JDL or other boy friends, we simply did not confide with each other about any matter relating to our girlfriends, it was personal to each one of us. Cyril and I had, at last, managed to coincide a week's holiday at the same time, and on the 18th with nine days to go, he met me after work and we began making the necessary arrangements. A couple of days after, on Sunday, we were on the beach at 8am with Dick, Monty, Frank, together with the indomitable sisters, Phyl and Bet, and it was probably at this meeting that we mentioned our prospective camping holiday and persuaded the girls to visit us at Spithurst next Sunday. We left the beach an hour later and met up again in time to play some tennis before dinner. It was past three o'clock when I cycled to Cobden Road to meet Cyril and we both peddled to Spithurst with the object of inspecting the camping gear and to let Erne know of our plans. The tents and cooking utensils were now being stored in an old railway carriage which was in the garden behind the farmhouse; it was common practice for these carriages to find their way to such places when they were no longer serviceable as rolling stock. One of the tents required repairing so we made everything ship shape and then had a chat with Erne, Millie and the boys, before getting on our bikes and heading for home, arriving at 9.15 which was an hour after sunset; it had been a lovely day!

The next step was to arrange transport for our kit and stores, so I wrote to Mr Osmond, a carrier who operated around the area and had a contact address at the Druid's Head, a well known ancient pub in the town centre; we had used him several times over the years. Owen's father agreed to be the pickup point which was ideal as he had a shop in Islingword Road; so all was set for the kit to be collected on Saturday, 26th August and for Cyril and me to cycle over the next day when we would also meet Phyl and Bet who were to travel by train to Barcombe Mills station. In the few days before our start date the threat of war took a serious turn as Hitler was about to attack Poland, and there were frantic ARP preparations taking place throughout the town and country. However our minds were on the impending holiday and the plans went like clockwork; we packed the food and kit bags which were duly picked up by Osmond, and on Sunday Cyril and I served at the 8 am church service, then cycled to meet Phyl and Bet at Barcombe Mills station, from there we all walked to Church Farm and the camp site which was some three to four miles. The girls helped us pitch the tents, set up the camp fire and prepare the meals – dinner and tea – between times we walked about the farm and woods or lazed in the sun. In the evening we saw them off on the 9.45 to Brighton, then returned to the camp, stoked up the fire and sat by it for an hour, talking or just enjoying the stillness of the night, the nearly full moon with the stars in sky. Five years had passed since our first holiday here; we had grown up together to love this place and with seven days and six nights of camping in front of us, it was a great thought, full of anticipation and we were free spirits. Apart from John Bower, who was still residing here at the farm, there were two girls on holiday and also some local chaps who helped out from time to time; we palled up with all of them and some evenings visited the village pub, the Royal Oak at Barcombe where we drank pints of IPA although I was really under age for such a tonic.

On Tuesday night there was a full moon and the two of us sat by the camp fire throughout its hours, sipping cocoa at 2.30 and making porridge at six in the morning. After breakfast we gathered timber from the woods; there were always plenty of fallen dead branches and a lot was required in preparation of a party planned for the evening when all those from the farm were to join us. We slept a bit in the afternoon then made a suet pudding, using a packet of Atora Beef Suet, flour, and sultanas from the stores, mixed together with milk, rolled then covered with greaseproof paper, tied in a cloth and popped in a large can of water suspended over the fire. It was kept boiling or very hot for more than three hours and we were apprehensive when returning from a walk and visiting the farmhouse, but the pot had not quite boiled dry, in fact the pudding turned out to be marvellous with treacle and we were pleased with ourselves.

Getting ready for the party was a matter of scrubbing a sack of 42 potatoes brought over from the farm, making a stand for the prospective arrival of a four and a half gallon barrel of beer and slightly enlarging the area of the fire. It was dusk when figures were seen moving towards us from across the field and much hilarity as the party drew near complete with the barrel; all told there were twelve of us including the farmer, Erne, his wife Millie, and I should mention John, also Muriel and Kath who were the girls on holiday, while two other ladies/girls and three fellows along with ourselves made up the number. We ate the spuds when baked in the fire, drank the beer, sang a song or two, and talked and talked until past midnight. Never had there been such a gathering at one of our camps but this was not the only memorable event to happen during our last holiday together.

A trip to the river was a must, so on Friday we went to the village where I telephoned Brighton 2394 and spoke to Bet who was at work; this was to confirm our arrangement to meet the girls the next day; an hour later we reached the Anchor Hotel, hired a boat and paddled up to Isfield Church. We spent three hours on the river and returned in time to visit another village pub in the evening. On Saturday, after helping Erne with the hay, we met Phyl and Bet at Barcombe Mills Station in the afternoon and walked back to the camp. As on the previous Sunday they were good company and helped to cook the sausage and mash, but time again moved too fast although their train back was a little later at 10.25. We arrived at the station to find it was running 30 minutes late which gave us an opportunity to visit the Anglers Rest, a nearby pub, for a drink before we kissed them goodbye and set off for the camp. The dark clouds which had been hovering in the sky suddenly erupted into a terrific thunderstorm with lightening and torrential rain; we reached the farm soaked, not daring to go across the fields to the tent we stayed in the barn cat napping until 2.30 when all was serene, so we ventured to the camp site and crawled between the blankets in the tent. What a great day it had been but ending with a storm which seemed to be an omen for the bad news about to come.

At the campsite – Phyl washes up while Bet and Ken chat.

1939
The Later Months

War is Declared

When Cyril and I surfaced from the tent later on Sunday morning it was as if the storm we had walked through and our sojourn in the barn had been a dream. The sun was shining and the ground was fast becoming dry, we lit the fire and had breakfast before making our way to the farmhouse in time to listen to the wireless at eleven o'clock. For the past whole week we had neither read a paper or listened to the wireless, but had been kept more or less up-to-date with the news and knew of the ultimatum which Chamberlain had given Hitler; so it was, we were both together when hearing the speech, which brought our country in conflict with Germany for their attack on Poland.

I cannot recall how I felt at the time, certainly it was no surprise as the preparations had been leading up to the fact for a long while, and I guess my mind would have been a mixture of apprehension tinged with excitement. Our date with the wireless had taken precedence over going the church service during which the vicar, the Rev. Farrer, announced the news to the village congregation. However, we stayed around the farmhouse for a while then returned to the campsite, rekindled the fire and concocted a dinner with the remainder of the stores before starting to strike camp. Kath (Walter) who was on holiday at the farm with her sister, Muriel, came across the fields to help us clear up, pack the tents and gear, making good the fire area and burying the empty tins by the hedge. I must admit to having seen a lot of Kath during the week, not only during the evening visits to village pubs but on the Thursday we had spent several hours together walking to Newick and Piltdown a round hike of about twelve miles, while Cyril had gone to Lewes with John Bower. Kath gave me her address, which I noted in my diary – 82 Eswyn Road, Tooting SW17 and I promised to write.

Having missed attending the church service at Spithurst, Cyril and I did the next best thing before we set off back home, we walked around the church and graves as we had first done five years ago. It was not a very old church; having been built in 1880 on land given by the Sclater family of Newick Place with money donated by the Shenstone family of Sutton Hall; these two large estates adjoined each other. Similar to our home church of St Luke, the external walls were faced with knapped flint; which was common in the south. There was no electricity so oil lamps and candles provided the light and solid fuel the heat, a bell cote at the west end was novel and seemed more likely for a school.

Barcombe. Longford to Piltdown. c1939.

The country lane leading to Newick and Piltdown

It was its position which brought the sense of awe to the building with the surrounding churchyard containing numerous gravestones; the entrance faced a country lane bordered by ditches and hedgerows; one side of the churchyard was adjacent to Church Farm although spaced by a cart track and a small orchard, while at the other side there was a plantation of pines; a wood of various trees stretched along the rear boundary and this went back a long way to border the field of our camp site making it possible for us to walk through the wood to reach the Church.

There are many places of serenity and peace such as this, but St. Bartholomew's Spithurst was very special to us as it was our camp church; we left the hallowed ground with some reluctance for possibly the last time, to walk the few steps to the Farm where we picked up our bikes, and having bid farewell to our hosts and friends, we left for Brighton at 5.30pm. The town's boundary was reached an hour later and we were greeted by wailing sirens that turned out to be a test, but the blackout that soon followed was no test, it was for real; undeterred we met up with the others and went for a stroll along the seafront in the dark as we all knew our way about the town.

Spithurst Church, exterior and interior, 1939

I returned to work the next day, Monday, 4th September 1939, and found my part of the office occupied by an Evacuation Committee engaged in planning the intake of children from London, who were already arriving at the railway stations. Everyone was now obliged to carry their gas masks, and I volunteered for a course of lectures on gas, at the Ronuk Hall after working hours. Initially it was the blackout which seemed to affect our lives most, as at sunset all outside activity became impracticable and movement in the town was reduced to a crawl for road transport and pedestrians alike. This was not so bad for the youngsters of our group and even our parents, but oldies like our grandparents found it very difficult. Access to shops, pubs, cinemas etc., was adjusted to prevent exposing light when persons entered or left the premises, whilst some simply closed for business when it became dark. Our church services, along with those of other churches, were restricted to the hours of daylight, but the activity in our church hall was maintained, as we were able to black out the windows and the outside door opened into small lobby before going through another door to the hall – it seemed made for the purpose. The JDL hut behind the hall had only one window, which was easily fixed and this venue continued to be well used by us.

As the days went by we became accustomed to these changed circumstances, while the population as a whole were undoubtedly adopting a spirit of helpfulness towards each other. No one, including the girls, spoke of being afraid to walk about the streets alone in the blackout for fear of being assaulted; the thought never entered our heads. The digging of trenches and sandbagging buildings was apace in the daylight hours; windows everywhere were being plastered with crisscrossed sticky tape in the hope of limiting damage from flying glass in the event of a bomb blast. Air Raid Warden's posts were being set up; the one in our area was at the Pepperbox, a peculiar structure so named because it looked like one – a pepper pot is the modern name but when this was built, about 1835, pepper was dispensed from boxes. It was and still is a relic from a large estate of that time, a prominent feature situated near Queen's Park at a large road junction incorporating our church of St Luke, the church hall, and the local pub called the Beaufort. Our Boy Scout troop used to store their

camping gear and trek cart in the Pepperbox so both Cyril
and I had been inside; now with sandbags protecting the
entrance, it made an ideal Warden's Post for the walls were
strong and with ten small windows around the top there was
a good view over the town.

*The Pepperbox
near Queen's Park
now known as
The Pepper Pot*

This was the backdrop at this time for our group of
friends until events were to eventually force us apart,
meanwhile we did not look ahead that far and carried on our
work and social activities, which were adjusted according to
what transpired each day. My routine at Ronuk changed
inasmuch I was asked to take over from the gatekeeper
during his breaks which meant having the to sound the
siren if necessary, I was also given the job of taking the mail
to the Brighton sorting office after work each day but this
was no hardship as it was not far out of my way; the gas
lectures continued. I wrote to Kath Walter, as promised
when we met at Church Farm, and received an unexpectedly
quick response so I was very happy at that and we
continued corresponding. The tennis games came to an end
on Sunday, 17th September when most of the group played
on the courts in the morning, and this turned out to be the
last time we would meet here. In the afternoon it was the
Harvest Festival at St Luke's with flowers only due to the

war as fruit and vegetables were already being preserved while fish was also scarce. I then went for a walk with the latest girl friend, Joan Heather (Gilmore), who lived just opposite the church and whom I had known for some time; we were now going about together; smitten yet again! I noted that the Aircraft Carrier HMS Courageous was torpedoed and sunk off Southern Ireland on this day, although I doubt whether we received the news until later; it was my first recorded war casualty, and happened to be the ship that Cyril and I had been to see from the seafront on 2nd August 1937. A week later I was obliged to clear up my bedroom and move to a smaller room to make way for three evacuees from London who came to stay with us, fearful that the City might be bombed.

"*The Hound of the Baskervilles*" starring Basil Rathbone, with a supporting film "*Too Dangerous to Live*" was showing at the Regent Cinema in Queen's Road on the 3rd October 1939, so I met my parents after work and we went to see it – an excellent programme. This cinema, although old (1921), had been restored in 1930 after a fire and was Brighton's best and certainly the biggest with 3,000 seats. It also had a Wurlitzer Organ, which provided an exciting entertaining interlude for it arose from the stage with the organist playing his signature tune, and we then sung along with popular songs such as "*We are going to hang out the washing on the Siegfried Line*" before the organ descended again. The cinemas were popular and often had queues waiting in the dark for seats to become vacant; the doorman would then announce the number to be admitted, and once inside an usherette would show you to a seat - lighting the way with a torch. We were lucky to have a choice of at least eight cinemas and I frequently went to the flicks with friends or family.

At work, I attended the fourth Gas Lecture and there was instruction about bombs and explosives. My ex-girl friend Doris (Cooper) left the firm and went to live in Chichester, so I would not see her around the works any more. I was physically sick on Portslade Station while on my way home on Saturday morning (7th), although I went to church on Sunday in the afternoon and then for a walk with Cyril, Jonah and Monty; this was probably not a wise thing to do, as on Monday I was too ill to get up for work. My doctor signed me off for a week, which I spent indoors, and by Friday I had completely recovered. There were grave faces everywhere the next day, 14th October, upon hearing the news that a second capital ship had been lost with the sinking of the battleship HMS Royal Oak in Scapa Flow by torpedoes from a U-boat. We were only six weeks into the war and this seemed a great setback, made more so because this ship was actually in one of our harbours. I doubt whether the full casualty figure of 833 sailors was disclosed at the time but we soon learned of one individual, John Simmons who had been a choirboy at St Luke's. Although John was not one of our circle of friends I knew him quite well and so would Cyril, for he was also in the Scouts with us, and there was one memorable occasion when I had a confrontation, or in other words a fight, with him in the church hall. He was a year below me in the same Junior School, St Luke's Terrace, and would have gone on to their seniors until 1937 when he became fourteen. Then he went to work for Sainsbury's where, attired with a large white apron, he sold chicken eggs from wicker baskets, which were arranged outside the entrance to the shop. I named him the Sainsbury's egg boy, and did not even realize he had joined the Royal Navy and was serving on this battleship as a Boy 1st Class until the news of his loss reached our community. It is good to have been able to write a few words about John who appears as a name on the Memorial in our Church of St Luke, the Brighton Book of Remembrance in the Parish Church of St Peter, and also the Portsmouth Naval Memorial on Southsea Common.

We held what was to be the last JDL meeting, the 146th, on the following the day and this ended the long run which had started way back in 1935. Cyril, Jonah, Owen, Monty, Basil and myself met in the hut to discuss the future of the club and take stock of the situation. Vic, my brother, had been called up for the army, and Dick was working in London at the time, so they were no longer available. We agreed to discontinue the formal meetings and meet in the hut for the sole purpose of recreation, but on the last Sunday of the month we would try and get together to pay Cyril, the treasurer, a subscription of sixpence. Any other of our friends who came along with us, for card games etc., would be asked to pay two pence for the privilege. It was a very low key ending to our four years of meetings, which probably reflected the dramatic change in our way of life and our outlook over these past few weeks.

During the second half of October I finished the course of Gas Lectures, in the Ronuk Hall, and took a test of sorts which was merely answering questions about its detection, effects of the weather, gas proofing a room and mustard gas. My answers were acceptable and I was declared to be proficient but it seems the matter ended there, as I never got to know the object of the exercise. I was also upgraded to a better position so I left the correspondence room where I looked after the mail along with some filing and indexing. It was very much like a classroom with six shorthand typists sitting at two rows of desks with the manager at the rear, and the mail, filing and index clerks along one side. In the office the ladies wore blue overalls which distinguished them from the factory girls who had white overalls and bonnets. If it had not been for the clatter of typewriters, coupled with the bell pinging at the end of each line and the noisy carriage being drawn back, our room would have seemed like a public library for there was no extraneous chitchat; the only telephone in the room was contained in a kiosk so that its use would not detract others from their work.

The correspondence room at Ronuk Ltd

My new job was in the order room where I sat face to face with a girl, Evelyn (Townsend), and together we priced the incoming orders, mentally working out the calculations or referring to typed lists. We also had the job of counting the coupons sent in under the Ronuk Reward Scheme; the coupons had a point's value and were put in the tins of polish, so they were printed on greaseproof paper, which made them messy to handle when returned to the firm for gifts. I got on well with Evelyn and even asked her to the pictures, but she was two or more years ahead of me and probably thought I was joking. However, I was altogether happier at the move, which still included relieving the gatekeeper in the time office and taking the mail to the Brighton sorting office. I was again enthralled by Basil Rathbone on the 21st, when I met Owen and we went to the Grand Cinema, in North Road, to watch *"Captain Blood"*. His sword fights with Errol Flynn over the lovely Olivia de Havilland took me into another world, with no thought of the rather shabby interior of the building which had previously been a Variety Theatre; in fact I had been to pantomimes there before it was converted to a cinema in 1931. The Victorian façade seemed more in keeping with the original use, it was quite ornate with several dome shaped recesses and arches at either end which fronted passages where there were side entrances and exits. Trams used to run past on their way to the station, but the Council had converted the transport to trolley buses by the time of this visit; they started operating on the 1st September – it was almost as if they knew when the war would start.

The very next day, being a Sunday, we walked over the Race Hill until sunset. The blackout conditions were becoming accepted as normal and I had to remind myself there was a war on by writing in my diary for 26th October: *"Europe is in a mess. Poland has been defeated, Warsaw taken by the Nazis. Britain and France are left to fight Germany, so far so good."* On the 27th I wrote: *"German planes have lately been making attacks on the East Coast but without success. The British blockage on Germany is making the Nazis reckless. The weather has been too bad for action on the Western Front."* My! How very naïve I was.

The cinema was becoming a habit on a Saturday evening, as with another week behind me I met up with Jonah and Basil and we went to the Palladium to see Conrad Veidt in *"Spy in Black"* and Jane Withers in *"Always in trouble."* The Palladium was in King's Road on the seafront between the two piers, the Palace and West, and like the Grand it had been a Victorian Variety Theatre with a similar but much smaller ornate façade, although this was completely replaced, during the 1930s, by flat slabs incorporating an art décor design; the interior, however, remained much the same with plaster designs looking like icing on a cake. We came out of the cinema at nine o'clock, there was a full moon which glistened on the sea and outlined the piers as we walked along the unlit promenade; the multitude of light bulbs on the piers and those strung from the lamp posts were extinguished for the duration. Parting company at the Pepperbox, I arrived home forty-five minutes later, little prepared for the surprising news which tomorrow would bring

It was not quite the usual Sunday morning at the Church on 29th October 1939 for this turned out to be our vicar's last service at St Luke's. After seven years, the Rev. Oscar Brooks announced he was leaving to become Chaplain to the English Community in Kobe, Japan; all the boys who had been with him throughout this time felt very sad, for he had been a mentor during our vulnerable teenage years which in my case was between the age of ten and seventeen. He preached his last sermon, said his last blessing at the close of the service and invited us into the vicarage for a get-together; it was here he ruffled our hair or patted our shoulders with affection while seeking promises to keep faith with the church, help our elders, and to write to him in Japan. Later on, after lunch, we met up again and donned our cassocks and surplices ready for a group photograph with the vicar, which was taken in the vicarage garden. Not everyone could be present for this event by any means; the "boys" aged twenty plus were, like my brother, in the forces, while for some reason only three of the older men turned up, so perhaps news of the photo call did not reach them. Nevertheless twenty three of the choir including Cyril, Jonah, Owen, Dick, Frank and myself lined up, with the vicar in the centre flanked either side by the curate, the Rev. G. Foss, and the organist, Herb Elliott. Also in the line were the two churchwardens, M. F. Chambers (my father), and Mr Collins who sat next to the verger Mr T. Hudson. 'Uncle' Bartley our assistant organist still had his bushy moustache and was at the back managing to peer over Cyril's shoulder. The camera set on a tripod was operated by a gentleman who traded under the name of "Baguel, Press Photographers of 56 Toronto Terrace", which was close by, and whoever arranged this very rare event for our church would probably never have envisaged the historical record that was being created.

St Luke's Church Choir, October 1939

The Rev. Brooks left for Japan four days later and I had hoped to see him start his journey, but my train from work did not reach Brighton Station in time. It was only a difference of minutes so my father, who had accompanied him, waited for me and we walked home together, via the GPO to deposit the firm's mail; my parents would miss the vicar as he often called at our house for a chat and to sample the bread pudding or cakes, but time does not stand still.

Badminton started, playing every Tuesday evening in the church hall; this took the place of tennis and was organized by Phyl who collected an agreed subscription of five shillings, and also five pence each evening to cover the cost of the shuttlecocks and lighting. My girlfriend Joan did not join but often came and watched, I was seeing her frequently for she worked in Vokins, a department store in the town centre, where I would often meet her from work and we would walk home together.

"*Belgium, so far neutral, is getting worried by German troops moving on their front.*" This was a brief note I made on the 6th November, followed shortly after by another reporting a big air fight between German and French planes in which the Germans lost nine aircraft and the French none; these figures plucked from somewhere, perhaps from a newspaper, obviously caught my attention for they were in our favour. I may have been taken back in time to 1929 when I played in the street with other boys of my age. We were either cowboys or Indians, dashing about firing cap pistols or, if we were not so equipped, our imaginary guns by just pointing fingers and shouting "bang." The Indians wielded invisible hatchets and twanged bows with arrows, then as the battle raged we staggered wounded or faked death, an indisposition which lasted a few seconds before we were alive and kicking to fight again. Our enactment of the German and English air battles involved running around like mad with our arms stretched out sideways, chasing each other while making zooming and screeching noises punctuated with the odd burst of chat, chat, chat, chat: no one ever got shot down but if our arms collided we sunk to the ground like damaged butterflies, only to take off again for another skirmish. My lead soldiers, at that age, were also a mixture of Tommies and Huns - the Germans had always seemed a natural enemy.

However that was just a fleeting memory of a decade ago, and a much more recent one was forthcoming in the mail, when I opened a letter from Kath and found she had sent me a photograph showing her sister Muriel, with some friends on holiday at Jaywick Sands in June 1939. It was a happy carefree holiday scene like many I had watched while lazing in the sun on our Brighton beaches, and although I was disappointed she was not in the picture herself, it was pleasing to receive the keepsake which, in any event, would remind me of the time we spent together during the September camp. I reciprocated by sending her a photo from a previous camp, and bemoaned the fact that our meeting had not been recorded by the box camera.

We played our first game of Monopoly in the JDL hut on 10th November when Cyril, Jonah, Owen and I, were joined by Monty who had purchased a set with the club funds. The game was invented by an American in 1934, so had been available in the shops for some time and it was Monty who suggested we buy it for he could get a discount. He duly appeared with the box and board, which was then unwrapped and set up, the rules studied, the first dice was thrown, and we were soon completely absorbed with the various situations the game presented and the hours flew by.

Kath's sister Muriel with friends at Jaywick Sands

A note in my diary suggests the clocks were turned back an hour on the 18th November, a Saturday, which was strange considering that Summer Time ended on the 8th October; this may have been a wartime adjustment, anyway it was the day we met again at St. Luke's for the wedding of the churchwarden, Bill Collins. I don't think any of us knew him very well although he had been with the church for a long time, nevertheless with the exception of Monty, who was not in the choir, we all turned up, donned our robes, sang some hymns and no doubt helped make it a successful event for him; the younger boys would have received a shilling for attending. I rather liked being in the choir at weddings for we had a splendid view, from the choir stalls of the bride and groom taking their vows and exchanging rings. Afterwards, in the evening, I went to the Odeon Cinema in West Street with my parents and we were back there again exactly a week later, but this time also accompanied by my girlfriend Joan. The film we watched together was "*Goodbye Mr. Chips*" which was a real tear jerker. This particular cinema had about 1300 seats and was only two years old; therefore it was a comfortable venue in a popular area of the town, and once again there was a full moon as we left the show which greatly helped us while returning home in the blackout.

After just three months, the blackout and the presence of sandbags, air raid shelters, wardens, police and others in uniform carrying gas masks and steel helmets had become common place; the war seemed distant and we continued to pursue our desires and activities regardless of the fighting across the Channel, in fact I gave up referring to it in my diary. The blackout was responsible for me tripping over a railway lamp towards the end of November, when I raced up the platform to board the last coach of a steam train which nearly missed stopping at Portslade. I suffered cuts to my knee and hand and felt more of a fool than the discomfort; it was fortunate the Ronuk mailbag did not fall on to the track, but I was able to hold on to it and the mail was safely delivered to the Brighton sorting office as usual.

A postcard arrived from Canada, sent by Oscar Brooks while en route to Kobe, so I started writing a letter as promised, I knew Cyril had already written to him for they had been very close. Our new vicar, the Rev. Graham Barnett, was inducted at St Luke's by the Bishop of Chichester on Saturday, December 16th; it was fortunate the proceedings ended before it became too dark in the church to read the hymn books! Although a New Zealander, he had been resident in this part of the country since 1932 and, like Oscar, he was a bachelor. The Church Council had asked the Bishop to appoint: "a man of moderate views and churchmanship, who would carry on the existing traditions and forms of service - a good preacher such as one having a fluent delivery, and would hopefully maintain a spiritual atmosphere with an aptitude for work among young people." He appeared to fit the bill and my first impression was that he was a very nice man, but we still missed Oscar Brooks. By this time, however, the JDL were well into organizing the Christmas party for Boxing Day. It had been just a mere thought at a gathering in the hut on Sunday, 10th December 1939, but five days later Cyril, Owen, Jonah and Monty called on me at Dawson Terrace and we got down to arranging the details. We no longer took minutes so the proposed menu and games for the event on Boxing Day were not recorded, nevertheless come what may, we were determined to have a good time; and invitations to the girls were sent out on the basis of one girl each.

I belonged to an unusual Christmas scheme in operation at work which was to pay a certain sum each week from January to December. The amount paid was split into units of one penny, thus my payment of sixpence resulted in six units, and in December they would be worth four shillings each. The firm would then use the funds to purchase, at trade prices, chocolates, cakes, perfumes, wines and spirits etc., in a quantity to match the number of units taken up by the employees; some items would cost more than four shillings but none would cost less than two shillings and six pence. The items and units would be numbered and put into a draw and then distributed accordingly, with the result I would receive six respectable presents and with luck get back more than I paid. It was a great idea, as I would always have something to give away at this seasonal time; chocolates to pass around or such like, and our party was an ideal event for these niceties. The scheme ceased to operate after 1939 as the war made it impractical.

A week before Christmas, Cyril and Owen turned up at my house one evening and helped put up decorations, holly and mistletoe, which gave the hall and rooms a festive look. I was pleased to have the morning off work on Saturday 23rd, as I went into town early for the purpose of buying some sausages at a butchers shop aptly named "Skinners"; no doubt they were for the party, and I waited 35 minutes in a queue before being served. I returned home in time to help our evacuees to the Coach Station and see them off to London at 10 o'clock; a large number seemed to be going home for Christmas and I felt they would probably not return because the expected threat to their safety had receded. Later in the day, I met my father from work which was unusual and so worth a mention. He was a master baker, pastry cook and confectioner by trade and had been working at a local baker's, John Botting, in St.George's Road since 1912. The mixing and baking bread, *et cetera* would start at four in the morning and he would always walk to the shop. It was a busy time for the bakery and he had asked for a hand to bring home the quantity of cakes and bread which he offered to provide for the party, and also extra for our needs to cover the holiday period, so I was happy to oblige.

At the morning Service on Sunday, Christmas Eve, it was nice to see Dick there as he was home on holiday from his civil service job in London, and would be able come to the party. His attendance was not expected when drawing up the guest list, thus in the hope of finding a girl for him to partner at short notice, I met Cyril, Jonah, Owen, Monty and Dick in the morning on Christmas Day, and as previously arranged we set off to see Phyl, and meet her friend, Joan (Nutley) who lived at No. 4 Belle Vue Cottages. This is one of a row of eleven cottages situated on the Racehill, along the west side of the Bear Road Reservoir which, unknowingly, I was destined to frequently visit. It was no coincidence that the tennis court we played on during the summer was on the opposite side, for it was through Phyl's friendship with Joan's family that we obtained the use of this facility. These dwellings are quite unique, standing out in isolation at the top of Bear Road, so named after the Bear Inn at the bottom of the mile long, poorly lit steep hill (1:10) which is flanked on either side mainly by cemeteries and was little used except on race days. We duly met the girls and Joan agreed to come to the party so our long walk was worthwhile.

The two weeks of anticipation came to fruition on Boxing Day. Owen and Dick arrived at 3.30 and helped prepare the food. Then Cyril's mother, my aunt Lottie, turned up to advise that Cyril would be unable to come as he had hurt his leg and was not feeling too good; this was disappointing, but as the others started to arrive; taking their coats off and briefly warming their hands at the fireplace, the party atmosphere began to be felt. There were fifteen of us including my parents and it was a very happy friendly time, in fact we did not disperse until more than seven hours had passed, at 12.30am All the girls were accompanied home and Joan Nutley had two escorts to see her safely back across the Racehill to Belle Vue Cottages, they luckily had a full moon to assist their walk.

My first thought when I awoke, after several hours sleep, was to visit Cyril, so when the house was made shipshape from the aftermath of the party, I packed some left-over goodies in a bag and set off for 54 Cobden Road. It was a pleasant surprise to meet Owen and Dick there and to see Cyril looking quite bright although hopping around on one leg; we kept him amused by playing crib for an hour before leaving and going on to the Grand Cinema to see Boris Karloff in "*The Mystery of Mr. Wong*". The Christmas holiday had come to an end and there were now only four days left in 1939; snow was on the ground when Jonah and I visited Cyril and the afternoon was spent with a walk along the seafront with my girlfriend. Jonah and I visited the Grand Cinema for the second time within four days and the programme was now "*Dodge City*" starring Errol Flynn and Olivia de Havilland with another film "*Wolf Call*". It was a rather uneventful ending to the year and I doubt whether the steam engines at the station sounded their whistles at midnight which was the usual custom. I slept soundly with little thought that tomorrow would commence a new decade.

Belle Vue Cottages where Joan Nutley lived

1940
The Early Months

On Guard at the Reservoir

January 1ˢᵗ was just an ordinary day, and at home in the evening I looked at my new diary, a Collins No. 134, which had a page a day roughly 2½" x 3½" and many pages of information. I noted the first Bank Holiday would be on Good Friday, 22ⁿᵈ March, postage remained at 1½d up to 2oz, telegrams were nine words for 6d, and telephone charges depended on the distance, the cheapest being up to ten miles for 3d. I carefully filled in the Personal Memoranda, the size of my collar 14½" and my gloves were size 8, and so forth. There were addresses and telephone numbers; then I came to the first day's page and wrote "*It is a pleasure to write in a diary like this which was a present from Wyn and Chas*" my sister and brother-in-law. What the other 365 pages would contain was yet to come, but I had no crystal ball and was not unduly worried.

On Saturday 6ᵗʰ I took the Christmas decorations down, spent some time with my girlfriend and went to the Savoy Cinema with my parents to see Bob Hope in "*The Cat and the Canary*" and "*Golden Boy*" with Paulette Goddard. The Savoy was a large cinema with 2,300 seats and it had a Hammond organ which vied with the Wurlitzer at the Regent Both had decorative coloured lighting and arose from the stage with the organist playing rousing tunes as part of the entertainment. Summer holiday makers could well have been attracted to this cinema for it had a commanding corner position on the seafront, nearly opposite the Palace Pier. However this was winter and we came out to a bitterly cold pitch black evening, but it was at least dry, so with the aid of our torches we gingerly set off walking home, arriving at nine thirty. Cyril was back on his feet by the first weekend and we served together at the early morning service on Sunday.

Sweets were beginning to be in short supply, but my job with the firm's canteen accounts enabled me to obtain two dozen 2d Cadbury's chocolate bars for 3s 1d. I brought them home on Tuesday, 9ᵗʰ January and it was a pleasing discount for my father who wanted them for the choirboys' treat. I was lucky to get the chocolate, as only the day before food rationing had begun with the distribution of ration books by the Ministry of Food; these were issued in conjunction with the National Identity Card which everyone had been obliged to obtain at the start of the war. National Registration Offices had been set up at that time and everyone was given a registered number and a card bearing their name and address; any changes had to be reported to the office when the amendment would be duly endorsed with a stamp similar to that of a post office. The Ration Book was valid for the year of issue and contained pages of coupons which were a mystery to me as my mother looked after the rations; I think she had to register with a butchers etc., and stick to the same supplier. I never had any worries about food and guess the family managed alright, helped a little by my father's trade, together with the fact he kept chickens and rabbits and had an allotment which could be reached in five minutes from over the rear fence of the back garden.

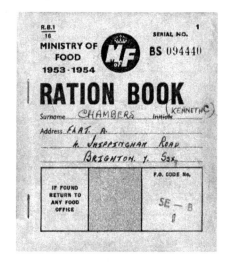

It was about this time I received the first letter from our old vicar, now in Japan, with the address: All Saints Chaplaincy, 53 Nakayamate-Dori, 3-chome, Kobe, Japan. The two closely typed pages were dated 30th December and so had taken six weeks in transit; I read the letter many times over, and regret it is too long to relate all but the gist:

"*My dear Ken ... very pleased to hear from you this morning ... unable to gratify your desire to be the first of the lads to write ... already had letters from Cyril and Arthur Pickering ... your letter is the quickest to have reached me ... posted December 2nd at 5.50pm ... to get to Kobe within the month is a record ... from the time I left England I missed you lads more than anticipated ... although we are now on different sides of the world we can still keep in touch by correspondence ... learning to live under different conditions ... to be rude to a policeman in Japan is to commit an offence against the Emperor who is regarded as a divine being ... I trust if the Japanese censor examines this he will not think that I am poking fun at a national custom or I shall be for it ... cyclists and motorists travel at great speed ... dodge all over the place ... narrowly missed being knocked down ... if I should have the misfortune to be injured and taken to hospital ... there are no beds Japanese sleep on the floor ... patients supply their own nurse and food ... men, women and boys do physical jerks at 7am in the street to music and instructions from the radio ... only 700 English people in this huge town ... learned to rely more upon myself ... can be lonely indoors ... I have a housekeeper she can't speak English and I can't speak Japanese ... never fear that a letter from you would bore me ... I was always truly interested ... your happiness and welfare and that interest has not lessened but deepened now that I am no longer with you to hear ... from your own lips ... remember me to all the JDL and to your family ... I trust in spite of these sad times you are well and happy. Your sincere friend O.E. Brooks. P.S. I wish you would call me "Padre" instead of Mr, even if the word does mean "Father" I am a father to you in more senses than one ... also it is less formal.*"

There is no wonder we all thought so much of the Padre because he thought so much of us. There was a Church Social on Wednesday evening, 17th January, when we all turned up at the hall and mingled with the older generation; admission was by ticket so there was a small charge, which possibly paid for refreshments and also the three musicians whose tunes enabled some of us to shoe shuffle around the floor. These events were very well patronized as it made a change for many, who may otherwise have sat by the fire at home listening to the wireless. It was unusual for me to visit the cinema alone, but on the following Saturday I went to see the Crazy Gang in a film called "*Frozen Limits*" which was showing at the Academy in West Street; I loved comedy shows which was undoubtedly the attraction. The Academy was one of Brighton's older, cheaper, cinemas located in a prime position between the Odeon and the Regent, and all these places of entertainment were on the straight main route from the Railway Station to the seafront.

Brighton railway station platforms...

...and concourse

I was well accustomed to the station as I used it daily; the Victorian iron and glass canopy covering the platforms and concourse always impressed me. The wooden indicator board was also fascinating to watch, with a clock face above each perpendicular section which was set to show the time of a train's departure, this was followed by the platform number, and the stations of destination; the latter being displayed on a system of shutters, activated by some mechanical means, which clicked into place like a fruit machine. It was almost as if someone was behind the board pulling levers, in fact should one of the slats operate incorrectly, a railway man was on hand to adjust it with a pole. When coming out of the main entrance into Queen's Road there was usually a smell of salty air wafting up from the Channel, and this was the route I took to the sorting office with the Ronuk mail; barely a five minute walk along the road before turning off into North Road where I delivered the bag at the huge Post Office building, which was nearly opposite the Grand Cinema. In normal times, during the summer, thousands of day trippers would be walking along Queen's Road, crossing over the Clock Tower junction, and continuing down the gentle gradient of West Street to the beaches; on the way they could buy buckets and spades, kiss me quick hats, and on the way back purchase china knickknacks and Brighton rock for gifts. Unhappily these holiday days already seemed a thing of the past with some shop windows blacked out, and sandbags around the police box at the Clock Tower.

I was at the Academy again on the next Saturday, this time with my parents to see Spencer Tracey with Richard Green in the film "*Stanley and Livingstone*", also Lew Ayres in "*The Amateur Detective*". We were home fairly early in the evening amid freezing conditions and awoke the next morning to even worse. The ground was completely covered with ice and many times on my way to church I had to crawl along on my hands as it seemed impossible to keep upright, nevertheless after the service the ice provided a great amount of amusement for all of us. On Monday I was obliged to walk to the station through a covering of snow, and then found the train service was also disrupted so I was late to work. It continued to snow throughout the day and no trains were running so I left the office early and walked about one and a half miles to Hove Town Hall, which was half the distance to the sorting office in Brighton; then I managed to get a bus to the Clock Tower and went on from there to deliver the mail and walk home. Even the next day, Tuesday, 30th January, there was a three foot drift of snow outside the house when I set off for work and again the morning train was delayed but at least the roads had been cleared and I was able to bus all the way to the Clock Tower and get home in good time. It was upsetting to learn that Monty had been taken into hospital with pneumonia; the news was so sudden.

Transport was nearly back to normal on the last day of the month, and I was at the church hall where the young people had been called to a meeting; except for Monty all my friends were there and it was decided to form the St Luke's Young People's Club. It was likely that we had Phyl to thank for this initiative, as she chaired the meeting and became the secretary.

It was now February 1940, six months into the war and the pages of my diary still did not reflect upon the fighting which was taking place across the Channel; I was more intent on the leisure time outside my working hours, which during the evenings and weekends appeared to be more or less unaffected. On Saturday afternoon, 3rd February I went to the Temperance Hall in Middle Street with Jonah and Basil; a strange title for a billiard hall but it is scrawled in my diary. It was Jonah's idea, so he led the way along the seafront and up Middle Street for a short distance before going down some steps at No. 7A which led into a large hall containing a dozen or more billiard tables. I never knew it existed, but the building on top of this underground cavern was the very well known Sherrys, or the Palais de Danse which was a popular Brighton night haunt that stretched across to the parallel West Street thoroughfare where there was another entrance. Sherrys dance band, with tables around the floor and more on a higher level overlooking the dancers, made it a very lively venue, especially after a few drinks from the bars.

Jonah was obviously familiar with the billiard scene beneath Sherrys, although I was not very impressed as it all looked rather seedy. The bright lights suspended over each table picked out the green baize and made the surrounding area appear dim, the air was thick with tobacco smoke, and the combined noise of the balls being struck during the numerous games was quite prominent above the near whispering of the player's voices; everyone seemed too serious for my liking. We paid at the entrance desk to cover an hour and were allocated a table number, then collected cues from a rack on the wall, set up the balls for snooker and started playing; the one hour was extended to another half hour of billiards before we left, and I was back home in time for tea. It had been a new experience for me.

On Sunday I learned that my girl friend was ill with measles and not wishing to call on her I wrote a note. It seemed there had recently been a cooling off of our close friendship, but for some unknown reason I was not unduly concerned. During the following week I was most upset when the Secretary at Ronuk called me into his office and complained about my hair. He said he had observed me playing table tennis in the hall during the lunch break, and how I tossed my head back to shake the hair from my eyes. It was an indirect way of telling me to get a haircut, because my mannerism was considered to be unbefitting for a member of the staff; I left his office somewhat deflated and it altered the way I felt about the firm. Perhaps I wanted to console myself or emulate Cyril, as I bought a pipe and started smoking Four Square yellow which was an excellent tobacco from a ½ oz tin.

It was good to meet up with John Bower, who came over for the day from Church Farm on Sunday, 11th

February. John was my oldest friend as we had started school together on the same day, way back in 1927, therefore I enjoyed this opportunity of a few hours together and, after tea, I saw him off on a train back to Barcombe and spent the rest of the evening in the hut playing Monopoly. His visit must have sparked Jonah into discussing the prospect of camping over the Easter weekend, as Good Friday was not far away. I was certainly interested although Cyril was not keen; I suspected he had a girl friend who worked along with him at the dairy, and having been in the same situation I well understood how he felt. While at the youth club on the following Friday evening there was a heavy snow storm and by 10.30 it was quite deep, nevertheless when I left the hall with Jonah we still seemed set on camping over the Easter holiday.

We arranged to check out the situation at Church Farm on Sunday. Fortunately, by then the snow had all but disappeared so we met up early and caught a train which got us to Barcombe Station in thirty minutes at 9.05. This station was on part of a single track, branching from the line which served Barcombe Mills, and the train driver had to collect a baton from the signal box at an earlier junction, which was a safety measure for ensuring there was only one train on that section at the same time. It was a less frequent service than at Barcombe Mills but nearer to Church Farm, and it was a nice bright morning in which to walk to our destination; I had not been to the farm since camping with Cyril last September, while for Jonah it was even longer, so it was good to be back and after greeting Erne, Millie and John, we went to the old railway carriage where our equipment had been left. We found the tents and blankets in a poor state for apparently Kath's brother Bob had used them at some time and not bothered to store them properly afterwards; luckily we had a hiking tent at home so would manage if necessary. The rest of the day was spent walking in the country with John, and he then saw us on the train back to Brighton.

The next day I had a chance meeting with Joan at the Pepperbox, and it marked the end of our association although we remained friends. It seemed odd for we had been so much together since last August, but suddenly the spark died; I would never really understand what went wrong.

We had a lively evening at the Club on the following Friday, when thirty of us turned up to debate the question – *"That the town is better to live in than the country."* The town won the day which was not my choice; and as we left the hall a full moon was lighting the sky but I had no girlfriend to share it with. It was decided that next week's meeting would be a musical evening, and I opted to join Owen, Frank, and Bert (Hoare) in a quartet to present a party piece. The four of us met in the vicarage room the next afternoon to practice our song and I noted it sounded terrible; I now have no idea what we had chosen to sing although it was most likely to have been humorous such as an extract from a Gilbert & Sullivan operetta. Later, in the evening, I was surely at a loose end for I went to the Kemp Town Odeon cinema in St. Georges Road to see the films *"Let's be famous"* and *"Mr Motto in Danger Island"*. This cinema was only six years old with about 900 seats and was set apart from the town centre, for Kemp Town was the name given to the eastern area of Brighton where some very impressive houses were built in the 1820s. However a little further east, a large council estate of over 1,000 houses had been developed, in Whitehawk valley, so this cinema would be near to these.

On Sunday Jonah, Cyril and I met up again with the intention of visiting Monty, who was still in the General Hospital, formerly the Workhouse/Infirmary situated at the top of Elm Grove just across the road from the grandstands of the racecourse. At one time this forbidding complex of grey buildings, surrounded by a high brick wall, would have stood in isolation overlooking the town below, but houses had long since crept up and around Elm Grove to join it. Our good intentions were thwarted as no visitors were allowed due to an infectious disease that had broken out in the ward, so we joined up with Owen, Frank, Phyl and Bet for a walk along the racecourse to Wrights Farm.

The farm was on the south side and half way along the horseshoe shaped course which followed the ridge of the hill, from this point we could look down Sheepcote Valley to the sea. Unlike the preceding view which was the Whitehawk housing estate, Sheepcote was open grassland sweeping seawards with a park at the end adjoining a secondary coastal road. Nearer to the farm, in the depth of the valley, were three large man made hillocks which were in fact "rifle butts" built for use in a past age and where, as a boy, I spent much time playing among the discarded water tanks, oil drums and corrugated iron which littered the butts.

Wrights Farm at the top of Sheepcote Valley

At the badminton evening on the following Tuesday I heard the sad news that Owen's mother had died after a long illness. This seemed to affect us all and Jonah, Cyril and I discussed a wreath as a tribute. The quartet with Owen, Frank and Bert was duly performed at the Youth Club's musical evening on Friday, 1st March. Everything went according to plan and we sang songs interspersed with our set pieces grouped around an artificial fire consisting of long thin logs arranged in a pyramid and lined with red crepe paper, under which a light bulb was placed to produce a cosy red glow. It was good to see Monty at the eleven o'clock service on Sunday, he was now out of hospital and Dick was also home for the weekend so we all had a walk along the seafront before lunch, then met up again in the hut during the evening.

A significant event early in the month was the fact I started wearing spectacles which were a great improvement to my sight. I took to them quite well and immediately tested them out by going to the Odeon in West Street which was showing "*The Under-Pup*" with Gloria Jean and a supporting film "*Mr Pym of Scotland Yard*". Preparations for the Easter Camp with Jonah started early with arranging the menus which we estimated would cost about eleven shillings, but Thursday the 14th was a very wet day which then turned into a blizzard with more snow; certainly not the weather to be in a field under canvas. Thankfully the snow soon melted and renewed our hopes that all would be well so we went ahead with shopping, then two days later Jonah's friend Alec drove us to Church Farm with some of the camping equipment.

I was still corresponding with Kath but had no special girlfriend and it was not surprising, that Jonah and me had a brief friendship with two girls, Iris (Brodie) and Betty. They were evacuees billeted with Mrs Trulock, one of our Mother's Union ladies, and they accompanied her to the church which was how we became acquainted and were able to date them several times. One very amusing occasion was on Monday 18th, we met at 6.30pm and while walking along the seafront it started to rain so we took shelter before returning. It was 8pm when we arrived back to their billet and Mrs Trulock was at the door waiting to give us a right telling off for keeping them out late. We did our best to make amends with her and my diary note "*Better late than wet through*" was a thought best left unsaid. They returned to London on Good Friday having reached the age limit for evacuees which brought an end to the brief friendship.

A couple of days before setting off for the camp we met Dick who had obtained a very necessary groundsheet from London, it was a nice size 4½ x 6ft costing 3/8d, and thanks to good friends like Dick we were now fully equipped. On the Thursday I went to work as usual then hurried home; Jonah called for me at 6.45pm and with our rucksacks we bussed to the station and took a train to Barcombe; this meant changing at Lewes but I was able to phone Barcombe 63 and contact John at Church Farm who met the train and helped us back along the country lane to the Farm. Fortunately it was a clear and starry night with the moon in our favour.

It was quite late when we arrived at our destination, and we called into the farmhouse to see Erne and Millie who must have thought we were mad to be camping so early in the year, yet alone arriving in the dark, but they were probably used to our spirit of adventure. We located the gear in the railway carriage and John helped us pitch the ridge tent in the far corner of the home field, which in the circumstances was easier to reach, and it was midnight before we settled down between the blankets amid the surrounding silence and the familiar smell of the canvas.

Ken's railway ticket to Barcombe

Making a fire was our first priority when we surfaced the next morning (Good Friday); we dug a hole after carefully removing the turf for replacement later, then collected dead branches from a wood bordering one side of the field, and in next to no time a billycan was boiling eggs for breakfast. We were mindful of the blackout regulations and in order to lessen the light of the fire when it was dark we erected a flysheet above the grate and were careful to keep the fire to embers. It was great to be at the farm with no thought of time, lending a hand if need be or just basking in the environment. We were joined by John in the evening and he stayed chatting around the fire until 10.30pm, then he left us to continue cherishing its warmth for a further three hours before we retired to the tent. Saturday was uneventful, the weather was much the same as the previous day; we walked to Barcombe and came back with some sausages which went down well with mash; it must have been a spur of the moment alteration to the planned menu. I felt the symptoms of a cold and retired early after 'wooding' which was the term we used for the constant need to seek out suitable dead timber for the fire, Jonah came in the tent four hours after me, at midnight, he had been sitting round the embers like the Lone Ranger.

Easter Sunday turned out to be our best day when we attended Spithurst Church for the early Holy Communion Service. Breakfast back at the camp was the usual Shredded Wheat and an egg, and later we were joined by John for the morning service at eleven. As I left the church with its surrounding graves I recalled walking here with Cyril last September and thinking then I would not be returning, yet here I was again with Jonah and I felt strangely fortunate in being the one who was at this peaceful place in turn with each of my original JDL friends. Perhaps there was a chance we would get an hour or two here again before the world events overtook us.

We walked to the village inn, the Royal Oak at Barcombe, and were rather idle when getting back to the tent so our dinner of corned beef and peas was not consumed until well past four o'clock; unfortunately we found the treacle suet pudding required boiling for an hour which made a long wait between courses. The day was rounded off with a party of seven including Erne and John visiting a pub in Newick, where we had a jovial time playing darts while drinking a pint. A lovely night's sleep saw us through to late Monday morning; we finished up the remaining rations, busied ourselves packing the kit, dismantling the tent, replacing the turf and making the site appear as though we had never been there, then I picked some hazel catkins, a sure sign Spring was bursting forth, before John helped us to the station for the journey back home.

The last day of March was a Sunday and we all played truant from the morning service to go to S. S. Brighton which was a sports stadium in West Street, a large and popular venue originally built as a swimming pool but changed to an ice rink in 1935. It later became the base for the ice hockey team, the Brighton Tigers but at this time other teams were playing and the object of our visit was to watch the Furies play the Spitfires; we went to these games many times, Cyril was a fan and I recall he had the bottom half of a hockey stick on the wall of his bedroom; this having been recovered from one of the players. In the afternoon I walked to the church hall to put up a poster advertising a youth club Social to be held on Wednesday; while on my way back home I happened to meet Audrey Lloyd who lived at 6 Dawson Terrace, the opposite side of the road to our house. We commenced chatting and ended up by walking along the seafront which was the start of another romance.

April 1940, I met Audrey again on the 2nd; it was a badminton evening but I came out of the hall early so that we could go for a walk along the seafront and from that time on, until the 9th July when she left Brighton, my diary was filled with my infatuation for her. She had dark hair and eyes - the complete opposite to my former girl friend - neither was she sporty and did not mix with my friends or go to our church, nevertheless I managed to spend a lot of time with her without neglecting too many of my usual activities. We would meet almost daily and more often than not walked around the town and to places in the surrounding area up to a four mile radius.

I received another long letter from the Padre; dated 16th March 1940 thus it had taken four weeks in transit. He appeared to be more settled in Japan and wrote:

> "*Most of these lads are Eurasians – I am hoping before long to start a club for them, but apart from the chaplaincy there is no building to hold meetings in – the news got around the school that the Padre had said some of them could come round after and play "Buccaneer" (they love that game and I am thankful I brought it with me) I was in the middle of my tea when the door opened and nine lads came in. As only six could play I shot out the others – we shared the tea but I had very little sugar and most of them like a thundering lot so they were unlucky – they enjoyed themselves and went home happy – three of them had a train journey of ten miles – the previous night I had six lads from the Canadian Academy to supper and they played Buccaneer.*"

It is a coincidence the Padre mentioned the game of Buccaneer for I had just acquired one to play in the hut as an alternative to Monopoly. The 'board', contained in a cardboard tube, was a large roll of cloth-backed paper which represented the sea with home ports, and there was a separate box which had a fascinating array of playing pieces - a tray to fix in the middle of the board which was the "Treasure Island" – the treasure, six of each, consisted of gold bars (brass), miniature wooden rum barrels, pearls, diamonds and rubies set in metal mounts – real quality fakes – there were six little ships of different colours with matching paper sails and wooden masts – lastly there were packs of special cards which provided the players with their sailing distance on the board and the fighting strength should one ship attack another – the objective was to acquire treasure and take it back to the home port and in so doing there were many different facets to the game before the winner was able to accumulate the required value of treasure. We all had some great entertainment with this new game when meeting in the hut.

Ken's game of Buccaneer

The Padre mentioned he had been invited to be the special preacher at the English Church in Tokyo on Trinity Sunday in connection with a musical festival service; this would involve an 800 mile journey and he was going by sea to Yokohama and on by train from there. His reference to the church and his housekeeper were amusing:

> *"The congregation is about twenty to thirty in the morning and fifty to sixty at night on Sundays – the communicants are seldom less than twenty – we wear Eucharistic vestments and I have two servers – the latter I am informed are given to*

*faint in the hot weather – I am told the Chaplain
usually perspires very freely in the pulpit in the
Summer – when I look up at the roof and see the
three big electric fans there – I do not look forward
to the Summer in church. I still can't speak
Japanese at all but manage to do all I want – my
Armah has not acquired any more English but she
manages very well – I have just made her
understand that I have a visitor for supper
tomorrow night – she said something about soup
and something which I fancy had to do about
chicken but I don't know and don't care – she will
provide a decent meal – if she meant chicken it
will not be expensive because she will buy two
legs and leave the rest of the carcass with the
shopkeeper."*

There was an amusing postscript to the Padre's letter –
*"Tell your mother that if I had a radio and was permitted to
do so, I would now even be willing to listen to that rotten old
serial at 3pm. No one is allowed to have a wireless that can
get foreign stations, and Japanese music is atrocious."* He
also mentioned that English newspapers and magazines
could not be purchased in Japan and neither would the
authorities allow them in the mail unless they were sent
direct from the publishers. As the result of this I wrote to
the Daily Mirror to enquire about sending the newspaper to
Japan and received an immediate reply with a specimen
weekly copy which could be mailed for 26 weeks for the
price of one pound; then I met Cyril and Jonah and we had
the idea of asking for donations towards the cost which
obviously succeeded as within a couple of days I was able to
send the subscription.

It was Kath's nineteenth birthday on Tuesday, 9th
April and I sent her a card, our seven months of
corresponding was just a thread of friendship which was
destined to break at some point and all that remains is her
address in my diary. John had called on me unexpectedly in
the afternoon of the previous Sunday to tell me he was
leaving the farm, but I had made a date with Audrey so I
promised to get to Spithurst next weekend to see him before
he left. True enough, on the following Sunday I cycled to
Spithurst, in the company of Owen to bid John farewell

before we set off back home armed with bunches of primroses fastened to our handlebars. Apparently there was no longer any work for John at the farm and he was going to his parents who had moved from Brighton along the coast towards Dover.

The month seemed to be going by quickly. Cyril and I made some preliminary arrangements for camping over the Whitsun Bank Holiday then, when we met up on the following Wednesday evening at the church hall where the Club was holding a dance, surprisingly he came with his girlfriend Joan Sharpe. It was nice meeting her; the evening was a roaring success with 150 turning up to shuffle in the French chalk to the sound of the Metro Rhythm Dance Band which certainly took the blues away. I made arrangements with Cyril to spend Saturday night at my house as my parents were away for a few days. He arrived quite late at 9.45 and we talked and talked for two or three hours while sipping mugs of cocoa and nibbling biscuits and cheese, such was the bond between us. Sunday morning saw us up early, we both attended church to serve at the 8 and 11am services, then in the afternoon we had tea at my sister's house, together with his girlfriend.

The undercliff walk on a stormy day

The war was not mentioned in my diary, all my time was occupied walking with Audrey; our longer jaunts together took place at the weekends when we would often walk for some three hours. The eastern end of the town was ideally situated for walks as it was not only close to the racecourse and the Downs but also to the section of coast where the flat beaches of pebbles and sand abruptly turned into high chalk cliffs; this point was known as Black Rock because rocks littering the base of the cliffs are covered in black seaweed and mussels which became exposed at low tide forming little pools of water where shrimps, crabs, starfish and other creepy crawlies abounded.

It would have been extremely dangerous to venture far along the shore under the cliffs for fear of being cut off by the tide, but in 1930 the County Council had started constructing a sea wall along the base of the cliffs to prevent further erosion of the chalk face, and this included a walkway which stretched for three miles between Black Rock and Rottingdean, with just one access point at Ovingdean where there were steps. This unique walkway, some ten feet above the high tide level was completed in 1933, and opened up more beaches, many with the fascinating rock pools which at low tide safely provided hours of enjoyment. This area was frequently visited and includes some familiar place names so I have appended a rough sketch map for reference.

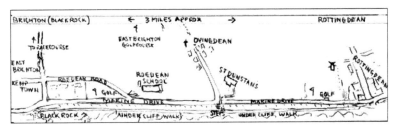

On Saturday, 4th May I went for a stroll with Audrey over the Downs to Rottingdean and back via the path under the cliffs. It was a fine day with a calm sea, but I recall many unrecorded times when the JDL members ventured along this path. We would pick a stormy day, more often in the winter, and brave the waves which lashed against the sea wall under the cliffs sending columns of water high in the air; it was possible to avoid getting soaked at the spots along the walk where this occurred by waiting until one wave had subsided and then hurrying past before another one arrived. Nevertheless we certainly became very damp with the spray and it was quite a job to keep my camera dry when taking a photograph of the scene.

"Holland invaded" - *"Belgium and Holland attacked by Germany – Bank Holiday cancelled - calling up from 19 to 36."* These scribbles in my diary on Friday and Saturday 10th/11th May were bad news, although it did not unduly worry me as I had great faith in being British. I was right in being dubious about camping over Whitsun although certainly did not expect this to be the reason for having to work as normal on Monday, but the buses and trains ran to time and I turned up at Ronuk along with everyone else. Arriving back in Brighton after work, still with the mail bag to deposit at the sorting office, there seemed more than normal bustle at the station and in the town due to the call to arms; the town had a large barracks in Lewes Road and two Drill Halls in Queen Square and Gloucester Road.

Two days later, Wednesday 15th, we had an air raid practice at work. There were no proper shelters and for most of us in the office it was mainly a matter of moving away from the glass windows, while those detailed for first aid and fire duties went to their posts. The firm had its own fire appliance, a hand cart containing a pump, hose reels, ladders etc., which were always at the ready as the factory handled much in the way of inflammable products. I must have somehow learned that civilians were being asked to volunteer for Defence Duty as there was speculation the country would be attacked by German parachutists and fifth columnists (sympathisers with the enemy) might cause damage to our utilities; consequently I called at the Town Hall, while on my way home from work, and put myself on the list without having any idea what I was expected to do.

I met up with Cyril and Owen on Sunday morning, as previously arranged, and we cycled to Newhaven nine miles east along the coast; an established fort on the high cliffs overlooking the port, now a military base. The purpose of our journey was to visit Cyril's father who was stationed there, or rather working there. He was a sergeant in army uniform but, like my father, he was in his fifties and I assumed he had just volunteered for particular work at the fort due to his skill in anything connected with water pipes and metal work.

St Wulfran's Church, Ovingdean

The evenings in May were now noticeably lighter; I was out and about after work walking with Audrey or with my long standing friends. The church had recommenced the Sunday evensong service at 6.30, and the youth club had started outdoor activities beginning with a visit to Ovingdean on Friday, 24th May, it was some way to our destination, the village church of St. Wulfran which was very old, dating back to the Saxons with some Norman architecture. We arrived at 9pm and met our vicar who had preceded us in his car. The sun had set and with no lights we would probably have not been able to see inside the church due to the black out regulations. Nevertheless it made a pleasant walk over the race hill to the end of the course, then by a footpath down a steep valley which led into the village; there may have been a shout of "four" en route as the path crossed the East Brighton golf links.

This visit reminded me of the old building across the road from the Church because my sister had lent me a book entitled Ovingdean Grange, a tale of the South Downs, by W. Harrison Ainsworth and published in 1857. The author lived in Brighton for 14 years, and resided at the far eastern end of the seafront where an estate of very large imposing terraced houses had been built. He would have had a good view of Black Rock from the windows of his house as it overlooked the sea; also Ovingdean was but a little distance along the coast and he went to the Church there, thus he inscribed the book to the "Rev. Alfred Stead, Rector of Ovingdean by one of his flock."

Ovingdean Grange

I thought Ainsworth cleverly combined fact with fiction in "Ovingdean Grange" which describes how King Charles II escaped to France after the battle of Worcester in 1651. History tells us the King met up with Nicholas Tattersell at the George Inn in West Street, he was the skipper of a coal brig and conveyed the King to France on 14th October 1651. However, it seems his stay at Ovingdean Grange, so lavishly detailed, was fictitious but because Ainsworth knew the area he was able to write a very plausible story. When Charles II returned to England in 1660 he honoured Tattersell with the rank of a Captain in the Royal Navy; he died in 1674 and was buried in the churchyard of Brighton's oldest church, St. Nicholas, where his tombstone with a long engraved inscription still remains.

My sister knew I would enjoy reading the book as it contained the reference to Tattersell which was the name of my house at the senior school; there were four houses all named after famous Brighton men, Fawcett, Godwin, Russell and Tattersell and we were allocated to one upon joining. Cyril was also in this school house and the story was of particular interest to us for our Great Great Grandfather Thomas and Great Grandfather Edward were married at St. Nicholas Church in 1826 and 1856 respectively.

At ten o'clock it was time to leave Ovingdean, some went in the vicar's car while others in twos or threes wandered down the lane towards the coastal road. I set off together with Cyril, Owen, Phyl and Bet, there were no lights but it was only three days past the full moon which was helpful. Within minutes we were nearing the junction with the main coast road and could recognize St Dunstan's, an imposing building on the hillside to our left. It stands alone, high above the cliffs, facing across the Channel towards the Isle of Wight and it was silhouetted by the moonlight. We turned right at the junction and headed for home, passing Roedean Girls School which was another impressive building, but out of sight a long way off the road beyond their playing fields and a brick wall which ran the length of their extensive grounds. My father often mentioned this school as the bakery where he worked was in the Kemp Town area and they supplied bread and cakes which were mainly the result of his handiwork. Finding a fish and chip shop in the vicinity of Black Rock was a stroke of luck, we were able to buy some chips, which we ate out of a wrapping of newspaper while walking the rest of way home. This particular British feast, although not rationed, was now usually reduced to chips only as fish was almost unobtainable.

Roedean School

Two days later, 26th May 1940, was my eighteenth birthday but there were no celebrations, just a normal day, except I received cards from my brother Vic, who had sent one from Belgium where he was stationed, my sister Wyn, Bet, Peggy, who was an old flame from school days, and the current girlfriend Audrey. It was a Sunday and Cyril, Owen and I repeated the previous week's activity by cycling to Newhaven to see Cyril's father; the sky was cloudy and it started to rain hard as we reached there but we found shelter in an army hut and Cyril's dad produced some very welcome tea. I noticed there was more activity around the harbour with many small boats but did not at this time realise their purpose; we never spoke about what his father was doing at Newhaven. The next day I received a birthday card from Kath which was no doubt her response to the card I sent her on the 9th April, so I take the blame for ending our communication. Maybe it slipped my mind because Audrey and I had a flaming row which upset me. On Wednesday I arrived at the sorting office with the day's mail as usual to find it was now under armed guard, they questioned my business and directed me into a nearby office where my details were recorded and I was given a pass; this enabled me to enter the building each day to deposit the mail. The GPO under guard indicated the increasing seriousness of the conflict across the Channel, but I don't think any of us yet realized the true gravity of the situation for our social activities continued as normal and with little mention of the war. At the Youth Club I met up with Cyril, Owen, Phyl and Bet, and along with the others we went into Queen's Park and played tennis; afterwards we returned to the church hall and had a dancing session to end another good evening.

The next day, June 1st, when I arrived home after work, my mother asked me to telephone relatives in Hove to let them know my brother was in England from Flanders; we did not have a telephone and my parents were not accustomed to their use, so I made the call from a public box. In the evening I went to the Regent, the posh cinema, with Audrey as we had made it up again and had seats in the circle watching "*Balalaika*" starring Nelson Eddy and Ilona Massey; there was a supporting film "*A window in London*" and of course a session with the Wurlitzer organ. During the performance I produced a box of chocolates; we had fun selecting them in the dim light; I was spellbound with her by my side and felt like a million dollars. The next day I was out with Audrey, it was a very hot day and we spent a lot of time just lazing in the long grass in the area of the race course where skylarks hovered overhead, singing all the time while on the wing then swooping down a short distance from their nests which they reached by walking through the grass, a ploy to deceive predators. There were also plenty of bees among the wild flowers growing profusely on the Downs, and the yellow flower of the gorse was out on bushes dotted about the hillside. Such was the idyllic scene just a short walk from our houses.

Two days later the carefree attitude of the last few days came to an abrupt end when I arrived home from work and heard the repeat of Churchill's afternoon speech to the House of Commons on the wireless. There was always silence when he spoke, everyone would listen so intently, and this was one of those times when his words would be remembered forever:

> *"We shall fight on the beaches, we*
> *shall fight on the landing grounds,*
> *we shall fight in the fields and in the*
> *streets, we shall fight in the hills, we*
> *shall never surrender."*

He was truly a great man whose mastery with words seemed to make everyone puff out their chest with determination and pride. I now grasped the significance of my brother's message that he was back in England, and also understood the purpose of the small craft at Newhaven which I had noticed when we there visiting Cyril's dad, they must have gone along the coast towards Dover for the start of the Dunkirk operation. By now it was over but during those days I had seen nothing of the activity as Brighton was some eighty miles from Dover.

It was exactly three weeks after I had put my name on the list for the Defence Corps that I received notification to attend the Drill Hall in Queen Square at 8.15pm on the following day, Thursday, 6th June. When I arrived I was asked for further details such as age, date of birth, occupation, hobbies etc., and this was entered on a form; then I was duly enrolled in the Local Defence Volunteers (LDV) and placed in Platoon 1 with instructions to report again on Tuesday 11th June, the whole process took 15 minutes. The day after enrolling I wrote in my diary *"The French are now resisting strong attacks by the Nazis towards Paris. Nazi planes frequently visit England but with little effect as yet. At Brighton here, the seafront is being strongly fortified with machine gun posts."* such was my vague view of the situation.

There was little any of us could do about the adverse war situation, it was a matter of carrying on as normal, at least for the time being, so I met up with Cyril and Owen at the weekend and was able to relate my enrolment for the LDV. Cyril informed us he had joined the Red Cross. We made plans to cycle to Bramley, near Guildford and set off on our bikes through Henfield and Horsham to Bramley where we spent some time with a pal of Cyril's. It was a very hot and hard ride of over 80 miles but nevertheless enjoyable for we took our time on the return journey arriving home in the early evening, so I was able to go for a short walk with Audrey.

On Monday 10th June my diary noted that Italy was now at war. The following day I reported to the Queen Square Drill Hall wearing the LDV arm band given me when I enrolled. The Platoon was transported in a variety of vehicles to Ovingdean where we were sub-divided into sections and I was allocated to Section 1. I have no idea why we went out of town, maybe it was a question of space because we were temporarily handed rifles and drilled for thirty minutes on the quiet road overlooked by St Dunstan's. Before being conveyed back to town our section was given instructions to report the next day to Rifle Butt Road at 8.30pm. The name of this meeting place could not have been more appropriate, it was a short road of less than a dozen houses which ran inland from the coast road at Black Rock, and may have derived its name because it was possibly the beginning of the path leading to the old Rifle Butts at the head of Sheepcote Valley; at this meeting I again met our section leader, who had the rank of a sergeant, and he told us we would be on night patrol starting next Monday, for my part he said he would call for me at 11.30pm.

The vicar proposed we should close the youth club for the summer but it was decided to continue our activities. On Sunday my brother came home on leave for a few days and although it was good to see him we did not have all that much conversation. *"FRANCE TO GIVE UP FIGHTING – ENGLAND LEFT TO CARRY ON AGAINST THE MIGHT OF GERMANY"*. I thought this important enough to use capital letters in my diary entry on Monday, 17th June 1940 although by now we were getting used to bad news; it was the date for my first LDV patrol and after seeing Audrey to make things right again after another argument I went to bed for two hours to get some sleep in readiness for the late night venture.

The LDV section's sergeant duly called for me at 11.30 when we set off walking to our allocated site for guard duty which happened to be the Bear Road Reservoir; while on our way I learned his name was Gerald Garratt and he lived at 79 Freshfield Road which was just around the corner to me. The night was fine and warm with the light of half a moon as we walked briskly up Freshfield Road and followed the race course round to the top of Bear Road; where the reservoir and Belle Vue Cottages stood out in isolation overlooking the town. I was never given any reason for the night patrol, I naturally accepted it was to prevent anyone interfering with the town's water supply and presumed all the reservoirs were now under guard; initially our section's watch was from 9pm until 6am in stints of three hours and together with Sgt Garrett we were to be the middle one. On reaching our destination the two of our section who were standing guard at the entrance gate challenged us, we made ourselves known, they handed over their rifles and left us to it. A shortage of weapons meant that only those on duty could be armed, the rifles were old P14s and with each rifle there were five .303 cartridges which we kept in the magazine. I had only handled one for half an hour, let alone never fired a shot, but I did not give it much thought as we were left to stand by the reservoir entrance for the next three hours. Fortunately I was familiar with being out all night when camping and also knew how to use a shotgun so my very first experience of guard duty with the LDV was taken in my stride.

I was back at the reservoir again three days later, this time on the first shift at 9pm with Doug Skipper who lived next door to me; we had called on the Sergeant to collect the rifles and the cartridges, which were in a clip as they had to be removed from the magazine when not on guard, and continued walking to the reservoir entrance where we loaded our cartridges into the magazines and watched the sun sink over the horizon in the direction of the Isle of Wight. Bear Road at this point ran alongside one wall of the reservoir before joining Warren Road, which followed the racecourse some way. before branching off into the valley leading to Rottingdean.

This was the only side of the reservoir that could be guarded as there were no footpaths around the remainder. It never once occurred to me that what we were doing must have been ineffectual, even more so because the gate was locked preventing us from patrolling the inside; nevertheless we walked back and forth along this section whenever we felt the need to take a stroll from standing at the entrance. My second tour of duty ended when Doug and I were relieved of our three hour stint by a couple who turned up fifteen minutes late.

At the end of the week I was yet again at the reservoir on the first shift and my companion this time was someone named Edwards who was a lot older than me. Walking back at midnight after a dull three hours I came to realise how the difference in our age limited our conversation, besides which all the men in the section were complete strangers having only met very briefly the previous week. Little wonder there were some awkward moments. Fortunately, I got on well with the Sergeant and that helped my acquaintance with the others – time would tell.

These late nights did not unduly affect my work or social life; the club met on Friday evening when the top news was the French surrender - an Armistice between the French and Germans was signed later on the Saturday which meant the Germans now occupied the ports across the Channel, and this circumstance accounted for the fact our beaches from the cliffs at Black Rock through to Hove were being made inaccessible by coils of barbed wire. The piers and the south side of the seafront road were all closed to the public.

A variation in the LDV activity took me to the East Brighton Golf Clubhouse the next Sunday, when I cycled there for 6 pm and met up with the platoon for ninety minutes of parade drill; this was the first of many Sunday evening sessions which I did not relish for nothing was being achieved. On this particular day I also had to guard the reservoir at midnight with yet another new acquaintance, a Mr. Coates, and we did not leave until 4 hours later, but any tiredness I may have felt was brushed aside as I brought my rifle home with me and then retained it throughout my time with the service. My mother was quite horrified at having a firearm in the house but I kept it out of her sight in my bedroom.

Bear Road Reservoir entrance and south wall

Cyril and our church curate, the Rev G. Foss, turned up on the doorstep the following Tuesday evening for me to accompany them in a run. I trotted along with them a few yards down the road to an area named Baker's Bottom where we picked up a narrow footpath taking us between the back of a row of old houses and allotments, it was a steep incline which joined a wider track running through the allotments known as Pratt's Lane. The allotments on either side were fenced by old cast-iron and brass bedsteads, rickety wooden sheds and greenhouses were dotted about amid the patches of cultivation. We came across several tethered goats that were nibbling at everything within their reach but they expressed no interest in us as we jogged past them to a higher level and the parallel stony Whitehawk Hill Road on the brow of the hill. There was a good view over the town and sea from this road (395 feet above sea level) which stretched from the end of the racecourse to the built up coastal strip, a distance of half a mile, where it descended sharply between the Sussex County Hospital and Brighton College both of which were only quarter of a mile off the main coast road. Our route took us alongside the college playing fields to the bottom of Dawson Terrace and we arrived back home after a run of nearly three miles in 15 minutes. I have no idea what brought on this one off exercise but the route to the racecourse did not surprise me, for I had often taken that path when accompanying my brother on a training run as he was a championship runner in the Sussex County Amateur Athletic Association.

Every moment of my time spent with Cyril was to become precious. We were together again three days later at the youth club and also Saturday afternoon when Owen and Dick joined us to play tennis in Queen's Park. In the evening the four of us went to the Odeon cinema in West Street and I returned home at 10.45 with only an hour to spare before meeting Jack Walker, another of our LDV Section, and reporting at the Bear Road reservoir for the third duty in a week. Jack and I stayed on guard until 4am and for the first time there was activity other than the sound of aircraft, we heard gunfire or bombs and watched searchlights waving about in the distance.

It was the 1st July, after work, when Audrey informed me the family were moving to Farnham on the 9th and I was very upset; the thought of losing her made me write many words of devotion over the next eight days during which I expressed the hope she felt the same and that being away from each other would somehow make no difference to our mutual affection. The days ran out like trickling sand in glass and we met at every opportunity; meanwhile the war revolved around us - air raid warnings with their wailing sirens had started to become a daily event so there was now no rush for the shelters which had been erected for public use – air raid wardens would don their tin hats and stand by, along with the other services, while everyone else went about their daily business - all hoping that nothing would happen. At work, if I was on relief duty in the gatehouse at the time of an alert, I would sound our siren on instructions conveyed by telephone from a control centre.

It happened that I was on guard duty the night before Audrey's departure, nevertheless I was able to spend the evening with her at her house before going to the reservoir where I stayed until midnight; she was looking out for me on my return and we had a few more minutes together before I crossed the road to 12A, my house – luckily our houses were opposite each other. Seven hours later we met up again for a short while before I went to work – the sand had run out on the 9th June and I was very unhappy. At work I had a rotten day because my mind was not on the job, although it helped a little when Audrey phoned the office at 11.15 to speak to me just before she left for Farnham. Two days later, early morning, I received a letter with her new address- "Kynance, The Fairfield, Farnham", and she appeared to be very unhappy so I sent her a telegram of consolation knowing it would reach her within an hour; in the evening I posted a letter at 8.15, before going on guard duty at midnight, this would arrive the next morning as the war seemed to have made little difference to the postal service.

1940
The Later Months

Preparing to Leave Home

I certainly did not mope at the weekend, although Audrey was still fresh in my mind; I went to the Savoy cinema on Saturday with my mother and we watched a couple of good films "*My Son, My Son*" and "*The Lone Wolf*". The seafront entrance of the cinema faced the coils of barbed wire which festooned the esplanade just a few yards away on the other side of the road, in fact work was still in progress on the fortifications along this stretch of the coast, which was still an unaccustomed sight and we missed being able to get on the beach and into the sea at this time of the year. Cyril called for me on Sunday and we met up with our other friends and walked to St Ann's Well Gardens in Hove, a distance of nearly two miles, an unusual place for us to visit but the seafront was out of bounds and we thought it would make a change from walking on the Race Hill.

The wooded area of St Ann's Well Gardens

I thought of Hove as being 'upper crust' and the gardens were no exception, there were the usual facilities for tennis and bowls, lots of flowers and bushes, but what made this park an attraction for us was the wooded area through which flowed the Chalybeate spring to a small secluded pond bounded by a rustic fence. In the 1830s a pump house was erected at the Spa which was visited by Queen Adelaide, the iron bearing water was said to be healthy but the popularity of this, unlike the spring, must have run its course for in 1935 the building was demolished. We had no thought of drinking the water but just enjoyed watching the fish in the pond, and the antics of the many squirrels in trees.

Without warning a lone aircraft dropped the first bombs on Brighton the following morning, Monday, 15th July 1940; these fell in the Kemp Town area behind the large Regency houses, damaging property and causing causalities in Whitehawk Road, Bennett Road and Princes Terrace. There were four gasometers fairly close by which bordered Rifle Butt Road and there was speculation these were the target but there was no knowing the pilot's intentions. I must have been travelling to work, in the opposite direction, at the time, and was told of the raid when I arrived. Our local newspapers published accounts and pictures of air raids but the locality was never mentioned.

On Sunday, 21st July I met up with Cyril, Frank and Dick and we walked to Roedean Golf Course. At the wooden shed alongside the course facing Marine Drive we each handed over one shilling and collected two irons, a golf ball and a score card, then proceeded to the first tee for the start of the 18 holes. We had very little knowledge of handling the clubs but made a fair attempt and it was great fun for two hours; I finished with a score of 94 although to win or lose did not matter in the slightest. Leaving the golf course, we walked along the cliff top to Black Rock where the main coastal road takes the name of Marine Parade and continues past the Regency houses of Kemp Town to the Aquarium and Palace Pier.

The lower road Madeira Drive was now closed and the barbed wire barrier fortifying the beaches stretched all the way to Black Rock, thus the scene greeting us from Marine Parade across these beaches towards the Palace Pier was one of desolation. We had heard the beaches were now mined and that gaps had been made in the piers to delay any attempt by an invasion force to use them.

Beach defence works and the Palace Pier, showing the demolished central span

In the evening we all had an important date which was to attend the church for evensong, this being the last time that our organist and choir master would be pulling out the stops and fingering the ivories of St Luke's Bevington organ; the church was packed as he was very popular. From my position in the choir stalls I could see the face of Herb Elliott in the angled mirror, through which he could observe the choristers, and it occurred to me I would miss him after having watched this reflection hundreds of times over the past eleven years. Perhaps Cyril, Jonah, Owen, Frank and Dick, who were in the same row, thought the same as we had always been in the south side of the choir (Decani) facing the organ which was installed behind the north side of the choir (Cantoris). Thus Herb Elliott could see our faces but only the backs of those choristers opposite us, and we had grown accustomed to watching the expression on his face and his body movements which at times amounted to conducting us. He was presented with a grandfather clock, and the vicar wrote this note about him in the August Parish Magazine:

> "It is with great regret and heavy hearts that we take our leave of Mr. H.B. Elliott as our organist and choirmaster; he has occupied that post with honour, devotion and distinction for 26½ years, before which he was assistant and a choir-man, and a choirboy before that – surely a record to be proud of. We thank him for all he has done for St Luke's, and wish him many more years of devotion as organist and choirmaster in the church much nearer to his home in Southwick."

On Monday, 22nd July 1940 I obtained my uniform at the Drill Hall, and this was also the day that Churchill announced the LDV was now renamed the "Home Guard". The uniform fitted quite well and I was impatient for an opportunity to wear it, which was not long in coming for I was on guard the following evening with Jack Walker from midnight until 4am. Earlier in the day I had received a letter from Audrey which as good as said that she had got over me, so I replied that she need not bother to write again – my hectic three months of infatuation with her seemed to end as quickly as it started but I was no worse off for the experience and had no regrets. Undaunted, a few days later I met a friend of Peggy Shipley who had been the first real girlfriend from my school days. We had remained good pals, with a hint of affection over the years, so it dawned on me to obtain her address from her friend as I now felt free to get in touch. She was in the Women's Land Army at a Forestry Camp in Culford, Suffolk and I lost no time in writing to her. Then I went to the Friday evening youth club meeting, proudly wearing my Home Guard uniform for the second time, but I had to leave early for I was on guard duty at 9.30pm and during this session Jack and I were visited by the Company Commander and Sgt Major – fortunately we were alert when they approached and after a few words they went on their way. This was certainly a one off occurrence.

About this time I received another letter, consisting of two closely typed pages, from the Padre in Japan, it was dated 23rd May and he had just received a batch of about twenty letters which included mine and two sets of weekly Daily Mirrors, so I was pleased to learn our subscription for this had not been in vain. I was privileged as he replied to my letter first, within three hours of receiving it, in spite of not feeling well after only recently having returned from his visit to Yokohama and Tokyo. The journey seemed to have caused him discomfort along with the humid temperature which made him feel like a wet rag. The Padre had travelled in a new Japanese liner to Yokohama where he preached on Sunday morning and then took a train to Tokyo where he preached in the evening. He continued:

> "It must strike you as a very long journey (750 miles) for the sake of preaching two sermons but one doesn't think anything of long journeys out

> *here – Kobe to Tokyo is referred to just as if it were a question of fifty miles or so – I did not see much of the Capital and thought Yokohama much cleaner – it has the advantage of being more modern, having been entirely rebuilt after the great earthquake demolished the original town about fifteen years ago. I was quite well on the sea journey – some fine scenery. The return train journey was tiring; eight solid hours of it with hardly a window open – the Japanese usually manage in a perfect fug but they don't wear as much clothing as we do and their feet are invariably bare."*

Then he changed the subject and complimented me on my handwriting, comparing it to Japanese which he thought was practically free hand drawing – it was unlikely he would ever learn to speak the language and had no wish to do so even though this caused difficulty at times. He ended with the words *"God bless and keep you all, especially the lads who always have and always will have the first place in my affections."*

A repeat of the previous Sunday morning was a game of golf at Roedean where we played better and Frank won by getting round the course in 84. I should mention that these jaunts were usually made after going to the early morning Communion Service, at which we took turns in serving, for it was rare not to attend at least one church service on a Sunday. We went to Gizzi's milk bar in the evening which was in King's Road, the main thoroughfare along the seafront where the large hotels such as the Queen's, Old Ship, Grand and Metropole were situated, whose sea views now consisted of empty beaches and miles of barbed wire but this mattered little for most, if not all, were taken over by the Military. Gizzi, an Italian, made himself a household name in the town with his ice cream which became as familiar with that of Wall's. Milk bars were popular places for us teenagers as it was a great feeling to sit on a high stool at the bar and be served with a milk shake. Flavours could be chosen like a cocktail from a range of bottles attached to optics, in similar fashion to spirits in a public bar, and whisked with milk and ice cream; it was pleasant to drink through a straw and while away the time in never ending conversation with friends to the sound from a jukebox. These were coin operated mechanical record players which obtained their slang name from America in the 1930s, Wurlitzer seemed the most common make and for a few pence the gaudy machine would play your selected record at the touch of a button; like all slot machines they must have been money spinners for the proprietors who hired them.

When I awoke to a sunny day on Monday, 29th July 1940, it was a good feeling to be on holiday for a week and the extra ten shillings, gift from Ronuk, in my pay packet was most acceptable. The holiday started well accompanying my Home Guard friend, Jack Walker, while he drove to numerous country stores delivering groceries – he was a van driver for Evershed's wholesale grocers who supplied a great number of shops in and around the area. His route actually included Barcombe, passing near Church Farm at Spithurst but there was no time to stop; at each port of call I helped with the delivery and there was a lot of paperwork involved due to the rationing. His round of about 100 miles took six hours and while on our way back the sirens sounded an air raid warning, but the all clear was given as we reached Brighton.

The next day I helped dad with the allotment; he grew nearly all his own vegetables in two plots amid the dozens in Craven Vale which stretched from the back of our house to the Race Hill, so they were within easy reach by just going over our back garden fence. In the evening I met up with Cyril and we went to the Gaiety Cinema to see "*Mr Smith goes to Washington*" starring James Stewart, Jean Arthur and Claude Rains, the secondary film was "*Flight to Fame*". This picture house must have been the last one to be built before the war as it was opened shortly after Easter in 1937, and was only about five minutes walk from where Cyril lived, in Cobden Road; we just walked down the hill to the main Lewes road then a little way in the direction of Lewes brought us to the our destination. The entrance to the cinema had taken the place of two or three old houses at the Hollingdean Road junction, and to make it look more imposing the concrete façade, illuminated with strips of neon tubing, was twice as high as the surrounding property. Of course the neon lighting had not been switched on since the start of the war, but this was of no concern as we entered the cinema and were escorted to a couple of the 1,400 seats by an usherette, who indicated the way with a torch. It was 10.40 when the performance ended and we left along with many others, including quite a number of army servicemen who went in the opposite direction to us towards Lewes, and it was my guess they were going to Preston Barracks which stretched for over a quarter of a mile along the west side of the Lewes Road. In fact, from this point, there was hardly any other property on that side until you reached Lewes about six miles further on.

The barrack block at Preston Barracks

We knew of the barracks very well, at least from the outside, for we passed by often when visiting our favourite haunts of Spithurst and the Anchor. It seemed to me to be a motley collection of buildings behind a brick and iron railed fence adjoining the pavement, nevertheless there was history behind the wall dating back to around 1800, and now, in 1940, our army was still mounting a guard at the gatehouse. No doubt some would be billeted in the barrack block without knowing it was one of the surviving buildings from over 100 years ago, when the occupants would all have horses to look after, for it was then a cavalry establishment with stabling for hundreds of horses. Many famous regiments must have been stationed there during those years but ours was now a different age. We had grown used to the motor vehicle which replaced horses, although there were still a few to be seen in the town and many more on the farms, which was just a well considering the present difficulty in obtaining petrol. Our mode of transport was the bicycle and my sturdy Raleigh was still on the go, looking better for I had recently fitted new drop handle bars. It did not have the three speed gear but did have a dynamo, which supplied power to the front and back lamps when it was twisted against the side of the back tyre. I had adjusted the front light to the regulation cross required by blackout rules by sticking thick paper behind the glass just in case I used it in the blackout.

I was on the bike before nine the next morning, Wednesday 31st, when I went to meet Owen who had agreed to accompany me on a ride to Farnham. The object was to visit my ex girlfriend, Audrey; it was more a matter of curiosity than of emotion as we had ceased communicating and it would certainly be a surprise. Without support from Owen I would not have undertaken to ride over one hundred miles on my own, so he was a real brick which portrayed the friendship our group all had with each other.

We set off at 9.30 under a cloudless sky. Our route took us a few miles north towards London before branching off west to Horsham, then further north-west past Loxhill and Milford, arriving at Farnham about 3pm We easily located the address and our knock on the door was answered by Mrs Lloyd, who was delighted to see us and invited us in for tea. Audrey was still at work so we did not see her but learned she had a new boyfriend who was not popular with the family. This news seemingly made our visit more welcome. Audrey's sister Mabel was at home and the four of us got on so well over tea we were asked to stay the night, but we were anxious to return and took our leave after an hour, setting off to Milford. From here we took a different route, turning south to Petworth then south-east to Pulborough, and Steyning where we joined the road of our outward journey, which brought us back to Brighton at 9 pm We had cycled a distance of about 106 miles in roughly 10 hours including stops for refreshments, but neither of us felt any worse for wear.

Upon arriving home I reflected on the fact that all the road signposts had been removed and in every village and town we passed any visible indication of their place names had been eradicated, so it was lucky we had carried a map. There were also huge concrete blocks dotted about here and there, no doubt placed in strategic positions to hinder the progress of tanks, and we also saw some pillboxes which had been erected near road junctions; these were some of the defences rapidly being put into place since the fall of France and the possibility the Germans would now invade us. However we saw no military activity and had passed by them with little worry as to their purpose.

The church club members met as usual on Friday evening and we went to Falmer, a tiny village just two or three miles out of Brighton along the main Lewes Road. Our destination was the Swan Inn, aptly named due to an attractive nearby pond which we walked around to admire the wildlife, before entering the hostelry which had a nice country atmosphere.

The next day, Saturday, I had nothing planned and was happy to accompany my parents and grandmother to the Savoy cinema. We watched the film *"North West Passage"* starring Spencer Tracy and I rather suspected the cinema to be a fairly rare event for grandmother, my father's mother, as she was eighty years old and did not seem to fully understand what was taking place around her. She had managed on her own since the death of grandfather in 1927, and remained at the same house (No. 8) Rosehill Terrace which always had a fascination for me with the grandfather clock and banjo barometer in the hall; while the living room mantel piece had material around the edge with tassels and supported a carriage clock and two candlesticks – it was like stepping back in time.

An air-raid warning on Sunday morning at 7.35 lasted twenty-five minutes so the church service started ten minutes late; these warnings were now becoming so frequent that I rarely bothered to make a note of them. I met Cyril and Jonah after the early evening Home Guard parade and we went to the Prince of Wales public house in London Road; the venue was Jonah's idea for he appeared to be more acquainted with pubs, although under age he certainly did not look it. I thought we were spoilt for choice as the Prince of Wales had half a dozen similar neighbours within a few yards in the same road.

This 500 yard stretch of the London Road was one of the town's three shopping areas, with a multitude of various shops on either side bearing the postal address of its route to the capital. All the familiar names, Sainsbury, Marks & Spencer, Woolworths, Boots and the Co-op, mingled with shops of every trade - butchers, dairies, fishmongers, coal merchants, drapers, confectioners, in fact anything could be obtained in this street and there was even a blacksmith's forge a few paces away, in a side lane at the beginning of an open market, where horses were shod and cartwheels re-treaded - always of interest to passers by.

The Parish Church of St Peter stands out as a prominent landmark, on an island at the southern end, where the road from Lewes joins the London highway and continues towards the seafront past the Victoria Gardens and the Royal Pavilion. My parents and Grandparents were married in this Church. The other end of London Road leads into Preston Circus, a junction of five roads reaching out in all directions and an ideal site for our fire station which was built next door to an old cinema, the Duke of York. This cinema's rather a squat ornamental façade with an unusual feature of a clock in the centre at roof level, and the double arched entrance porch under a balcony gives me the impression of an old time music hall or theatre rather than a picture house.

St Peter's Church

I recall the Preston Circus junction at northern the end of this shopping thoroughfare from the late 1920s for my grandparents lived nearby; it was the age before traffic lights and there were stop signs at the end of each road, like railway signals, operated by policemen from a box in the middle of the junction; the signal arm, bearing the word "Stop" was raised or lowered by a lever in the police box, so he could direct the flow of vehicles. Fortunately the arms were hinged, for I once saw a vehicle fail to stop in time and it hit the arm bending it back, the policeman came out of his box to berate the driver before adjusting the sign and resuming his work. However by 1940 there were electric traffic lights operated by the wheels of a vehicle passing over a pressure pad in the road, the lights were masked according to the blackout regulation; the police box had been replaced by a pill box disguised to look like a newspaper kiosk which the Home Guard would probably have the job of manning.

All the shops were closed as it was Sunday evening and it was a drab scene around the Prince of Wales where the three of us were at ease sampling the beer. We had become accustomed to things not being what they used to be, and in any event this did not affect our friendship or the beer. Along with playing darts and chatting we discovered that none of us would be working the next day. This was a stroke of luck for although it was the August Bank Holiday, at least on the calendar, it had been officially cancelled; we readily decided to spend the day on the river at the Anchor Inn.

I awoke to a beautiful sunny warm day and was soon off to London Road Station, meeting up with Jonah and Cyril on the way. Cyril suggested this station would be less crowded and indeed it was as there were very few people waiting on the platform. This railway station, the first of two between Brighton and Lewes, the other being at Falmer, is quite close to London Road at the end of a remarkable brick viaduct, constructed nearly a hundred years ago to carry an essential rail line east of the town over a wide valley and the major highway to the Capital. Although I hardly ever used the station, I knew it well due to the footbridge which connected the platforms and two residential roads, providing a shortcut to Waldegrave Road where my mother's brother lived, near to Blaker's park which was small and not often in the news but at least worth a visit to see the park's iron clock seemingly a Westminster miniature.

An electric train, bound for Eastbourne, soon took us as far as Lewes where we intended to change to a steam train for Barcombe Mills, on the Tunbridge Wells line, but found there would be a long wait so we set off to walk, following the river Ouse four miles upstream to reach the Anchor at midday. In no time a boat was made ready with

Railway Viaduct

cushions and paddles, we hopped aboard and commenced paddling on the stretch of water we all knew so well, the pleasure experienced during the next seven hours is nigh on indescribable as we turned the clock back to 1935 when the three of us discovered this idyllic place.

In spite of the war nothing had changed, the river was quiet, fish jumped up to catch the flies, water-boatmen skated on the surface, midges danced in the shade, dragonflies hovered by bank side flowers, kingfishers perched ready to dive for a meal, and the birds sang. Occasionally we rested the paddles and drifted, speechless, taking to heart the peaceful scene which had so much effect on our senses. Upon reaching the point nearest to Isfield Church we moored the boat, scrambled up the bank and walked across the field to renew our memory of the interior and the tomb of Sir John Shurley with his two wives and nine children, it had been there for nigh on three hundred years so our five years of acquaintance was infinitesimal, nevertheless we spoke in whispers and reverence as though they had died yesterday. Some time later we returned to the boat and headed further upstream to spend a while at the waterfall, before meandering back to the Anchor where we checked the boat in at 7.20, having spent seven hours on the river venture. A short walk following the river brought us to Barcombe Mills and finding there was not a train for an hour we visited another favourite tiny inn next to the station, the Anglers Rest, for a pint while playing crib until it was time for the train which brought us back to Brighton.

Back to work as usual on Tuesday, promising a busy week ahead as Evelyn was on holiday and the chair opposite me at the desk was empty. I was also on relief duty this week at the gatehouse or time office for this was where the factory employees recorded their working hours by inserting a card in a clock mechanism which stamped the time of their arrival or departure. In the evening I had a date at the vicarage along with Cyril, Jonah, Owen and Frank, we stayed a couple of hours discussing our church activity then went across the road to the Beaufort; the imposing public house which accompanied our church, the hall and the Pepperbox at this large junction. Jonah did the ordering for he seemed to know the barman and we each paid for our own drink, being well aware that none of us were all that wealthy. Although well accustomed to seeing the Beaufort this was the first time I had been inside, and there was no doubt it would not be the last visit; my age obviously had something to do with my lack of knowledge concerning public houses.

The Beaufort in Queen's Park Road

Guard duty at the reservoir with Jack on Wednesday night, and then came Thursday, 8th August when there was much air activity with planes often passing overhead. I spent four hours on duty at the Ronuk gatehouse and was obliged to sound the air raid siren several times, the engine noise made me look up every time in the hope of catching sight of the aircraft but I had little view of the sky through the window of the gatehouse.

The next day Evelyn rang the office and gave a week's notice so I was a bit apprehensive as to who would do her work when she left. On Saturday, after working in the morning, I spent a lot of time helping dad alter the chicken run in the back garden, he wanted to get another couple of birds, making the number to six as they were a great asset, producing eggs and the occasional nice meal. I was expected to be on guard duty at midnight, but it must have been a really tiring week and foolishly I decided to get an hour's sleep beforehand. I overslept and eventually opening my eyes at 6.00 on Sunday morning, however there were no repercussions and an apology was accepted. I don't think this mishap had anything to do with the warning given during the usual parade at the Golf Club in the evening, when we were informed by our sergeant to be extra alert as a consequence of increased German air attacks taking place further along the coast towards Dover; he also asked us to report to Brighton College the following evening for practice on their rifle range.

Brighton College entrance in Eastern Road

As I changed into my uniform after getting home from work on Monday, I was quite looking forward to having a go on the rifle range, so happily set off for Brighton College just a few minutes away in Eastern Road. I had never given this boys' school much thought and merely regarded it as being rather posh; I had seen some of the pupils in khaki so was aware of the cadet force and guessed this accounted for presence of the rifle range.

No one was in the sports ground as I walked past to meet the others at the college entrance; it seemed the whole platoon were there as we formed up in our sections and went through the archway to the range building. Only a few of us could fire at any one time so it was a case of waiting for my turn, then, along with Jack and a couple of others, we took our places in front of the targets. As I lay down with a .22 rifle and five cartridges the targets 25 yards away looked mighty small, however I was full of confidence as I stood up after expending the rounds. The others did the same and when we were all standing the targets were recovered for inspection. Alas my target was completely unmarked having been missed with every shot; there was consolation to learn I was not alone but it was still a disappointment as I was quite successful shooting rabbits with a shot gun at the farm.

The next day I travelled to work during an air raid warning which lasted an hour. These daily alerts had become frequent since the beginning of the previous week and I had to operate the work's siren more often when on duty at the gatehouse. Evelyn's notice duly expired on Saturday morning when everyone said their goodbyes; I was left to contemplate working without her, but the following Monday I managed quite well on my own. In the evening I set off with the sergeant for my third guard duty in eight days, a four hour period from nine o'clock. We saw the sun go down over the horizon to be replaced by a full moon, its light diffused by low thin cloud. Before long the silence was broken by the usual drone of aircraft overhead with planes flying back and forth on bombing missions. I suppose it was near midnight when, standing by the reservoir gate, our post was suddenly approached by a large number of men, coming towards us in extended line from the direction of the race course; their outline was clearly visible on the brow of the hill and we heard the clink of their equipment. My sergeant touched me on the arm and I followed his action; got down on one knee, opened the rifle bolt and pushed a round in the breech, then grasping the stock I accidentally grabbed hold of the trigger resulting in a loud bang, a flash from the barrel, and the bullet sped harmlessly into space. The effect on the men was magic – they all fell to the ground and there was a moment of suspense while everyone, including myself, recovered from the surprise, then a well educated voice called "Who's there?" and my sergeant shouted back "Home Guard, who are you?" The response was "I thought as bloody much" and an army officer, with his platoon grouping behind, came up to us; he ranted on about indiscriminate shooting and that someone might have got hurt, then marched off with his men after declaring the matter would be reported. About fifteen minutes later a dispatch rider appeared whom we correctly challenged with "Halt, who goes there?" He came with a message that there were Army manoeuvres in the area tonight – which by then was all too late. I am sure my sergeant was under the impression the shot had been deliberately fired over their heads. He told me not to worry, not that I would have done anyway, but it was good to know he would support me if need be. We passed the message on to our relief guard just in case the army put in another appearance, and set off together for our homes which where not far apart. After a few hours sleep I was off to work again, I liked my job and was never reluctant to catch the train to Portslade.

Tuesday, 20th August 1940 was memorable for another one of Churchill's unforgettable speeches; I was glued to the wireless hanging on to every word and bursting with pride to hear of the prowess of our fighter pilots battling against the Germans. As Churchill said: "*Never in the field of human conflict was so much owed by so many to so few.*" His speech and the newspaper reports were the subject of conversation when I met up with Cyril and Jonah in the evening and we again went to Gizzi's milk shake parlour in King's Road, now a favourite haunt - due perhaps to the jukebox. The air battles taking place further along the coast towards Dover were very much in our minds, the newspapers were giving daily the number of German and British aircraft shot down and the figures were running into hundreds. When we left Gizzi's the sun had set to be replaced by the nearly full moon, in a cloudless sky, silhouetting the coils of barbed wire along the promenade on the opposite side of the road. We followed this to the Aquarium where we joined Marine Parade taking us to a higher level so we could look down over the road and beaches from Black Rock to the Palace Pier; it was an eerie sight as the moonlight danced on a calm sea gently lapping the pebbles, there was no other movement along the desolate barricaded beaches – yet just a year ago the area, including the pier, would have been ablaze with coloured lights and densely populated. We turned inland at Rock Gardens and started the slight gradient to our destination, the Pepperbox, where we parted company after another of those precious times when the three of us were together on our own.

I did not have quite the same rapport with two friends, Ken Brooks and Sid Bartle who I had agreed to meet on the following evening; our common interest was being pupils at the same school in 1936/7. We met at the Fire Station in Preston Circus and decided to visit The Rookery, an ornamental garden along the main route towards London.

The Rookery

The Rookery is small but I understand it is large enough to vie with any such garden in the country, unique in design with tons of rock boulders strategically placed on a steep railway embankment. I recall its construction in 1935, as I often went to the park to participate in school athletic competitions, the rocks were unloaded from railway trucks and carefully slid down the slope to their required positions, steps and paths were made enabling visitors to meander among the rocks at various levels to reach the top of the embankment, from here one could look down on the London highway and across the valley to the expanse of Preston Park.

At the foot of the garden, level with the road, a large rock pool had been made with stepping stones which always created much amusement as each stone was big enough to support two or three people. The pool was alive with fish and water lilies, kept fresh through a cascade of water descending over the rocks in the centre of the garden, and with the addition of numerous different plants among the rocks the whole garden as seen from the road was very attractive, even more so at night when illuminated with coloured flood lights but these were now switched off for the duration of the war.

During this brief meeting with these ex-school chums I was reminded of our old boy's club which produced a news sheet called "Bison," an apt title for the Brighton Intermediate School's Own News. Jonah had been a member of the club and I occasionally went with him to play snooker and such like at their premises, which were in a large detached house in the grounds of the school at the southern end of Pelham Street. The building was a mystery to me except the ground floor where the social activities took place, and I well remember being there with him on one occasion when we were playing around with a golf club in the surrounding grounds; I placed the ball on a tuft of grass and gave it hefty whack, surprisingly it flew into the air over the iron fence and through the window of a house on the opposite side of the road. There was nothing for it but to apologize and offer to pay for the damage which cost half a crown, a tidy sum out of my pocket

On Sunday, 25th August there was variation to our Home Guard activity at the Golf Club, I cycled there at 10.15, expecting the usual drill, and found the whole company had been called together. We were assembled in our platoons and then set off across the precious golf course turf, all fanning out over the downland between Sheepcote Valley and Rottingdean; our platoon was on the left flank and by coincidence finished up approaching the Bear Road reservoir, exactly as the army had done six days ago when I fired over their heads; we then reversed direction to return down the hill and reassemble at the club house. It was difficult to understand the object of the exercise, unless it was to practice operating as a company or to test the fitness of the men, as most were elderly and the hills were quite steep but no one in our platoon had to give up.

I was back at the Reservoir on duty in the evening, from nine until midnight, with Jack who had become a frequent guard companion. He called on me and we walked together over the Race Hill; the sun was now setting at around eight o'clock and the moon was on the wane so it was quite dark when we took up our position. It was not long before the drone of aircraft passing overhead broke the silence, a familiar sound and although I always looked around the sky I had never yet caught a glimpse of one, not even when there was a full moon. We were about halfway through our spell of duty around 10.30 when our attention was drawn to the noise of an aircraft that came and went through the blackness of the sky in the matter of seconds; it was noticeably flying quite low. A few minutes later there was a glow in the sky from the direction of the town and Jack agreed that I walk to the brow of the hill to get a better view over the area. It took me only a few minutes to reach a vantage point and although there was plainly a fire in the town I was unable to pin point the position. Jack then took a turn but we were no wiser until our relief arrived at midnight, when we learned that incendiary bombs had been dropped on my old school the Brighton Intermediate School. It was a coincidence that only last Wednesday I had met up with the couple of my old school chums and we were recounting our reminisces of the BIS.

I was quite concerned as to its fate so I visited the area the following evening and from the end of the street, which was closed, was pleased to see the large Victorian red brick structure looking very much intact despite severe damage to the roof, fortunately the walls were thick and the interior floors and staircases were stone. Nevertheless as a result of the fire, four sections of the ornamental façade which supported the previous pitched roof and added height to the building were lost, regretfully spoiling the original Victoria architecture.

The Brighton Intermediate School

I did not stay long looking at the damage to my old school for sight seers were not welcome at scenes of destruction and often death; in any case I had a date at the Drill Hall in Queen Square to meet my sergeant as we had been summoned to appear before the Company Commander in connection with the shooting incident; the Army officer had been true to his word and reported the matter. We waited about fifteen minutes before being ushered into the C.O.'s office by a staff sergeant, there was no particular formality, it was just a case of walking up to his desk, standing to attention and saluting. He wanted to know our version of the incident and my Sergeant explained that our post had been approached by a whole platoon so I had fired a warning shot over their heads; if the truth was known I guess the officer was even a little amused, but he kept a straight face in telling us it was not the right way to act and we should have given the correct challenge which included the words "advance one and be recognized" when there was more than one person approaching. "Remember that in future" were the words which ended our short interview and we saluted again before leaving the office.

Jonah took Cyril and me to a different pub on Wednesday evening, 28th August, the Reeve Inn at the corner of Park Street and Eastern Road, its location just south of Queen's Park was well within our area. The attraction here was a room containing a full size billiard table which Jonah said was usually unoccupied, and indeed it was so we had a congenial game while sipping a pint, a nice way to spend an evening, but we had to leave early for I was on guard duty with Jack at 9pm.

While at work on Saturday morning I asked to see the firm's Secretary, Crescens Robinson as it was the end of the month and an appropriate time to tackle him about an increase in salary, justified by the fact I had been much busier since Evelyn's departure. He was very receptive although could not give an answer there and then, nevertheless I was very hopeful and it put me in good spirits with yet another guard duty in the evening, and having to be back at the reservoir again on Sunday morning, 1st September. The whole platoon had been ordered to meet at 10 o'clock when we were formed up and marched down Bear Road then along the Lewes Road to Preston Barracks, for anti-gas instruction which involved passing through a gas chamber. It was a refresher for me as I already had a certificate (pictured) for the course undertaken at Ronuk in October last year, but this time was different because I now had a service gas mask which was far superior to the civilian issue.

Anti-Gas Training Certificate

Heartening news on Monday morning when I was called into Crescens Robinson's room to be told he was recommending a salary increase but he did not mention by how much and when, I simply had to wait and see. In the evening I changed into uniform for a repeat visit to the Brighton College rifle range where I had better luck, hitting the target with all five shots and even getting a bull. The other four were not near enough to warrant a pass but at least it was considerably better than two weeks earlier. The exercise finished well in time for me to reach the Reeve Inn where I had arranged to meet Cyril and Jonah. Cyril stayed at my house the following evening and for some reason we busied ourselves cleaning the piano, a monster ebony black wooden cased upright which had stood against a wall in the front room ever since the family moved here on 17th April 1937. It had been transported from our previous address at 113 Queen's Park Road and had taken four men to manoeuvre the unwieldy object out of the old house and into the new, so the most Cyril and I were able to do was to bring it forward a few inches and dust behind, polish the woodwork and keyboard, then push it back. Mum was pleased with our effort even though it was rarely used, if at all, because none of the family could play it properly; alas I had been given a few lessons when I was about eight but created a fuss at having to stay indoors and practice the scales therefore dad rightly withdrew the 2/6d a lesson. We were treated to a drink in the Beaufort for our good work before Cyril returned home to sleep in my bed, while I donned my uniform and went on a guard duty from 10pm until 5am – the seven hour stretch was made possible because the Home Guard had taken over an empty property in Belle Vue Cottages and our section used it to rest or sleep between periods of patrolling the reservoir; it was a handy arrangement but did mean I rarely had much sleep.

Cyril, whose mother was away for that evening, stayed for breakfast and we set off early together for our respective jobs. When I came out of the Ronuk Hall after lunch, the sirens had just sounded a warning and upon hearing the roar of aircraft I looked up to see several planes flying at all angles, twisting and turning in a cloudless sky, the stutter of machinegun fire indicated there was a skirmish taking place which unfortunately moved out of sight towards the sea so I did not see the end result. It was certainly an unusual event to happen in this area but along the coast, further east, dozens of aircraft were fighting pitched battles nearly every day, the newspapers reported the numbers which became a sort of score card and fortunately we appeared to be winning.

A general meeting of the youth club at the church hall in the evening elected Phyl as secretary, Owen as vice president, Cyril and I became committee members along with two girls; there was a good turn out with much interest and it was now our job to arrange an activity programme. It seemed we had lost our enthusiasm for the cinema since we began visiting the pubs, nevertheless I went to the Savoy with Jonah on Saturday evening, 7th September, and saw *"Bulldog Sees it Through"* starring Jack Buchanan, the other film was *"Dr Kildare's Strange Case"*. The sirens sounded a warning during the show but no one moved. I arrived back home fairly late to learn that there had been some heavy air raids on London during the day. Once again I went to the golf club with the Home Guard on Sunday morning, our section had transport from the Pepperbox which saved a lot of time, as I had more or less given up cycling. We were shown some trenches which had now been dug at strategic places on the hills, they were not very deep, but did have sandbags around the top which were covered in turf which would have given some protection, nevertheless I was not informed of any plan for manning them in the event of an invasion. More daylight raids were taking place on London, although we did not know it at the time, but the following evening while on patrol we could swear to seeing a red glow in the sky towards London, the result of fires caused by the air raids since Saturday. The Germans had changed their tactics and were now trying to destroy the city, but the news reports on the number of planes being shot down was heartening. It seems hundreds of aircraft were flying over Kent and Essex, yet here we were just fifty or so miles away from the death and destruction which was taking place.

At the youth club we entertained ourselves by playing shadowgraph. This was someone's brilliant idea of suspending a sheet between two pillars, then fixing a light on one side so that objects between the light and the sheet produced a shadow, which was then watched by an audience seated on the other side. We took it in turns to have a go at making comic shadows with surprisingly amusing results, and for an hour or so it took our minds away from the serious German assaults on London, which had been the subject of Churchill's speech earlier that day Wednesday, 11th September. As always Churchill was a master of words in telling us of the Germans' attempt to destroy our ability to resist an invasion, and likened the situation *"to the days when the Spanish Armada was approaching the English Channel and Drake was finishing his game of bowls, or when Nelson stood between us and Napoleon's Grand Army at Boulogne; we have read about all this in our history books but what is happening now is on a far greater scale, and of far more consequence to the life and future of the world and its civilization, than those brave old days of the past,"* then he urged everyone to do their duty with special pride and care which was an echo of Nelson's signal to his fleet *"England expects every man to do his duty".* It was fortunate our country was an island with the English Channel again offering us some protection, and although there was nothing our little group could do, I am sure everyone, like me, lived with the certain faith in the prowess of our people to overcome this threat to our liberty and our way of life.

The following evening I had a rotten time on guard duty, along with Jack, it was very wet night with a strong wind and we were glad to get away after four hours, even then there was the unpleasant walk back home which took longer as we followed the road rather than cut across the wet grass by the race course. I climbed into bed at 2.30am but six hours later on Friday morning the blues departed when I learned from the firm's secretary my salary had been increased by six shillings and two pence, how the odd two pence came into it is inexplicable, nevertheless I was pleased and celebrated my new found wealth with Cyril and Jonah in the evening at the Reeve Inn. After lunch on Saturday I fell asleep in my room, and when I opened my eyes at 4pm it came as a surprise to learn that several bombs had been dropped fairly close by in the Kemp Town area; one in particular had hit the Odeon cinema causing many casualties including children.

Sunday was a lovely sunny autumn day so we all set off for the Roedean golf course. Our route along Eastern Road passing Brighton College and the Hospitals took us close to where the bombs had dropped the previous day. We had a glimpse of the structural damage when looking down the roads which branched off towards the coast road, one of these, Abbey Road, lead to the site of the Odeon at the junction with St. George's Road where there was much activity clearing up and restoring damaged roofs and windows. Continuing on our way we had a peaceful game of golf while unaware, at the time, that the greatest of air battles was taking place over the Thames Estuary as the Germans attempted to gain superiority in the air prior to launching an invasion of our island.

Jonah, Ken, Cyril and Frank at Roedean Golf Course

I arrived back home from Roedean at 2pm and gave no thought to the odd times of my coming and going day by day, my mother never once complained and somehow managed to produce or leave a meal for me when needed. She went out nearly every weekday to the shops, some of which she was registered with for rationed food, such as the butchers, and it involved a lot of queuing and checking the documentation before obtaining the allotted portion per person. No doubt similar circumstances applied to my friends who were back with me at 3.30 when we played various card games, three hours later we were in the choir at the church to welcome our new choirmaster and organist Mr Holgate who was taking the place of Mr Elliott. Perhaps it would have been advisable to have gone to bed after the service, but I whiled away the time before going on guard duty at 9pm with the sergeant. We met at his house in Freshfield Road and walked across the racecourse to the reservoir – a long night followed with cat naps at the guardhouse until 5am, then another cat nap at home before rousing myself for a day at work; the guard duty, at least three nights a week, was now hardly worth a diary entry.

Daily air battles and the prospect of being invaded seemed to hang like a cloud, under which life carried on as usual. The usual for me was my job in the Ronuk office producing accounts relating to the supply of polishes; this seemed of little help even though some of the products went to military establishments who wanted metal and stove polish among others. The firm also had contracts to supply and polish the floors in the wards of hospitals, which was done by a team of men who manipulated long handled weighted brushes over the wooden flooring; a tedious task but the polish acted like an antiseptic in keeping such places clean.

A hit and run air raid at the weekend, Friday, 20th September 1940, demolished a pub, the Lewes Road Inn at the junction with Franklyn Road. The attack took place in the morning and I did not hear about the incident until arriving back home from work. I was also at work when bombs were dropped the following Tuesday afternoon in Albion Hill, a very familiar street much used by me as I had walked down and up its steep slope twice a day when I was at the Brighton Intermediate School and lived in Queens Park Road. There seemed to be no particular reason for these spasmodic attacks which caused casualties and destruction, maybe they were stray aircraft from the air battles taking place further along the coast.

On Saturday 28th I met Peggy with whom I had been in correspondence for the past two months, she was home for the weekend from the Land Army at Culford, Suffolk; we went for a long walk and there was no doubt we got on well together so we arranged to meet the following day. On Sunday I cycled to Church Farm, Spithurst in the morning to see my mother who was staying there for a few days; it was always a great feeling to visit that quiet spot in the country which had so many happy memories for me. It was unusual to make this journey on my own but I was back with my friends in the afternoon and at the evensong service, before meeting Peggy when we went for another walk, which renewed our affection for each other, and we promised to keep writing.

On Monday, Jack and I were unexpectedly detailed for guard duty at a reservoir nearer to home, opposite the racecourse grandstands. During the 9pm to 1am patrol, in the moonlight, I noticed a difference in the construction of this reservoir's flint and brick walls; this one bordering Pankhurst Avenue was built with more embellishment than the others, possibly because it faced the General Hospital complex which stretched all the way back from its main entrance in Elm Grove.

The Resevior, Pankhurst Avenue

This reservoir was not as remote as our usual venue and the gate was unlocked, the guard post was just inside the entrance where a small hut had been erected to provide shelter from the elements. I suppose we could have walked around inside the walls but neither of us attempted to do so as we had not seen the area in daylight; we contented ourselves with taking turns standing by the door of the hut while one of us occasionally walked out on to the pavement and along the two accessible outside walls. It was unusual for us to encounter pedestrians walking about but we did so here, especially during the early part of the evening, and they expressed a "good evening" when passing the gate as if they were previously aware of the guard. Our four hour stint without a break, came to an end when the sergeant arrived with two of our section to relieve us, they had walked from the Bear Road reservoir so it seemed he had the task of arranging a guard for two reservoirs on this particular night.

It was now the first of October and air battles were still reported taking place towards London which had also suffered night raids throughout September. The newspapers printed a score tally of aircraft shot down, with pictures showing the wreckage which had been collected from around the countryside to form large piles of twisted metal, by all accounts most of it was German aircraft, and our faith in our forces was not misplaced.

On Saturday, 5th October, there was another variance to the home guard routine for I had to report to the Golf House at 2pm where the platoon was assembling to be transported to a rifle range at Balsdean. This was yet another downland valley, east of the road between Rottingdean and Woodingdean, and the area was completely new to me as our transport turned off the road just past Rottingdean, on to a narrow lane which ended up at the Balsdean water pumping station. Our destination was further up the valley along a cart track near to some deserted farm buildings where an outdoor twenty-five yard rifle range had been constructed with sandbags; we lined up and went through a similar procedure to that at the indoor range. I was thrilled at being able to fire my .303 rifle properly for the first time, and did quite well with my five rounds by getting two bulls, two inners and a magpie with my five shots, a total of 16 out of 20 – perhaps I should explain the "magpie" was not a bird, but the name given to the ring on the target between the inner and outer rings. An hour later we were on our way back to the Golf House, and at least for me it had been an enjoyable experience.

After arriving home from work on Monday, I was assisted by Jonah in moving a pile of bricks to the back garden as the Council was supplying the material to renovate our air-raid shelter – we then went to the Reeve Inn for refreshments. At some stage over the weekend I must have seen Basil Wooldridge and arranged to meet him on Tuesday evening, 8th October 1940, when together we went to see the YMCA official Mr. George Davey at their premises in the Old Steine. The object of the visit was to enquire and express an interest in joining their scheme for placing teenagers such as us on farms, to gain agricultural experience. I was very much attracted to the idea, mainly because of my love for Church Farm and the countryside which had played a large part in my life over the past six years; also I sensed my group of friends would soon be separated now that we were all in our late teens.

Basil and I were two of the eight likely lads who were present at the YMCA to learn about their Agricultural Scheme which operated under the slogan "British Boys for British Farms". Mr Davey explained that those who joined would initially be allocated to a farm as a trainee for ten weeks and then they would arrange suitable employment at another farm. It sounded attractive and we left in high spirits but there was a snag, our parents' consent was required and they would be asked to pay £7.10s towards the cost of our accommodation at the farm. When I arrived home and discussed the matter with them they did not share my enthusiasm, it took several days before they realized how much this meant to me and gave their consent, which set the wheels in motion; Basil also passed this hurdle so our applications were linked together.

During the second week in October I received another letter from the Padre, this was really special as he had also enclosed a photograph and commenced by writing, "*Owing to the heavy postage and risk of damage in transit I am only sending the enclosed to a few special friends, I must include you as, contrary to all reasonable expectations, you have proved a good lad.*" This remark made me feel privileged as he was no doubt referring to my letters, one of which was mentioned in his last communication as being ten closely written pages; these were compiled over a period of several weeks.

He continued, "*I hate being photographed, but it occurred to me that an ocular demonstration would constitute greater proof of my fitness than any statement I could make. It is very hot out here now but I seem to have got used to being in a constant state of perspiration. The mosquitoes are certainly a plague, but the only real risk from them is if they happen to seek a meal off you immediately after having bitten someone who suffers from malaria; however although I have been bitten many times I show no signs of malaria.*" Referring to the news that Roedean Girls School had been evacuated to the Lake District, and knowing that my father's bakery supplied the school, he jokingly remarked "*No more buns! How depressing your poor old papa must be.*" Lastly he penned a down to earth P.S. "*I now wear white clothing and an open necked shirt – can't stand a clerical collar at any price.*"

The Padre,
Rev. Oscar Brooks

     Our activity at the youth club evening on the 16th October was another one off event when I took the family's magic lantern to the hall to give a slide show. It is strange how objects react like old photographs in recalling the past; the lantern had been my grandfather's and, having recovered it from the attic for this event, I was immediately taken back to my childhood days in the 1920s when dad would set up the lantern for a performance at my birthday and Christmas parties. We would sit enthralled in front of a bed sheet hung on the wall awaiting the magic pictures which would suddenly appear, there were all sorts of suitable subjects such as Little Boy Blue, Hey Diddle Diddle, Little Red Riding Hood, Cinderella, then there were firemen, lifeboat men, animals and sailing ships; one slide in particular was about 12" x 2" which could be moved slowly through the lens to animate a hand painted comic train consisting of a teapot, six cups and saucers, a bottle, three red wine glasses and lastly a punch like man reclining in a gravy bowl, they were joined together and given wheels to produce a sense of motion to the objects.

     At that time, the light behind the lens was provided by an oil lamp with two or more wicks, so apart from being dim, the rear of the lantern became too hot to touch and filled the room with fumes, therefore I had every hope that a 'Heath Robinson' conversion to an electric light bulb would be satisfactory in the church hall. Cyril and Owen called to help me carry the equipment and set it up for the show which surprisingly went very well, the lantern's novelty made it a successful evening.

At the end of the following day I unexpectedly became 15 shillings richer when the Home Guard platoon attended a pay parade at the HQ in Queen Square; we were lined up in the Drill Hall and one by one approached a table to receive our allotted sum. It is strange that I had never given any thought about being recompensed for my time with them, which since enrolling in June had been considerable; neither could I recall any previous payments, so I was surprised to receive this money and did not know how the amount was calculated. Perhaps more important was the heartening information that the threat of invasion by the Germans had subsided, which was certainly good news, although their bombers were still out in force during the hours of darkness; we still had to be alert for enemy parachutists and saboteurs so our activities continued unabated. I heard that another one of our choir had been killed in action; Ron Sinden was lost when his ship, the destroyer HMS Venetia was sunk by a mine in the Thames Estuary on the 18th October 1940. He was about the same age as my brother, in his early 20s, nevertheless I knew a number of the older boys by virtue of their association with the choir, and Ron particularly stood out in my memory as he was a friend of my brother.

Basil and I had both received advice from the YMCA, requiring us to obtain a medical report certifying our fitness for working on a farm; we compared notes while digging away at the air raid shelter in the back garden. I had already made an appointment to see my panel doctor on Monday, he was Dr. Hinckley and I could not recall when I last saw him which was just as well for his surgery, in Florence Road, was a long way from our house. I duly visited Dr Hinckley on Monday evening, he took my blood pressure, listened with his stethoscope to my chest and knocked me on the knee with a rubber hammer, then declared me fit and said the report would be sent to the YMCA. I came away from the surgery with the pleasing thought that this was a little nearer to getting on their farming scheme and hurried home to tell my parents; finishing up the evening by playing crib with them and my grandma.

The next day I received a letter from Peggy, since meeting her a month ago we had been in regular correspondence and from the tone of our letters she captivated me as I did her, so we were well and truly together again, albeit from a distance. She had asked for a current photograph of me, so I called at a well known photographers, Jerome Ltd, who had a small studio in the town's main shopping thoroughfare Western Road; it was strangely sandwiched between a large drapers, called Dawkins whose window displays occupied much space on either side. The studio's window in the centre displayed recent portraits and local wedding scenes portraits could be taken immediately without appointment and as their prices were reasonable they were a popular name around the town, so I went there for Peggy's request.

Ken's portrait.

I hurried home with three copies of the photo which everyone thought was a pleasing result and posted one to Peggy, then I spent more time on the air raid shelter in the back garden as the Corporation had undertaken to deliver bricks, sand and cement the following morning and it was necessary to prepare for this. The shelter we had dug in a hurry two years before had been very makeshift, and the intention now was to enlarge the original hole in the ground to accommodate brick walls in place of the wooden shuttering, and provide an area about six feet square and six feet high with brick steps down to an entrance on one side; none of us realised how much work would be required for this upgrade, but the end was in sight. After a night on guard at the reservoir I got home early in the morning, slept for a couple of hours and was having breakfast when the lorry arrived with the bricks and materials which were simply dumped on the road. It was midday by the time I had moved everything to the back garden ready for the bricklayer. As before, the Corporation provided the materials without any cost and the rest was up to the householder, so my father had arranged for a local builder, Ben Napier, to do the bricklaying, he only lived around the corner in Queen's Park Rise and was also a member of our church community. My friends called for me in the afternoon and we walked to Roedean for a game of golf, it was quite a party with Cyril, Jonah, Owen, Frank and also Dick who was home on leave from an RAF unit where he was training to be a Wireless Operator/Air Gunner.

We met up again in the evening at Frank's house to play Ludo and Rummy; Frank lived opposite the church at 189 Queen's Park Road, he had suffered a serious illness when a young boy which left him with a damaged leg causing him to walk with a limp but he got about remarkably well. He was a good friend, the only one I knew who went to the Xaverian College, a private school only steps away from the church and occupying a large area enclosed by a mixture of high flint walls and iron railings which bounded Queen's Park Terrace, North Drive and Tower Road. This land was once part of a large estate within the confines of Attree Villa which now housed the college. Possibly it was Frank's disability which caused his parents to send him there and I considered his father, who was also in the choir, to be at bit aloof with an executive job at Evershed's a well known wholesale grocer.

*Xaverian College at
Attree Villa near
Queen's Park.*

On Monday, 28th October 1940 I noted that Greece
and Italy were now at war, we were helping the former and
the latter was hostile, it seemed a matter of fact statement,
almost an afterthought, as I did not immediately appreciate
the seriousness of this escalated conflict, in fact the next
day's news startled me more when I wrote "*Empress of
Britain sunk*". Undoubtedly it was the stately name which
caught my attention; it well suited the ship which was a
huge   merchant   vessel   that   also   carried   passengers.
Apparently she was north of Ireland and heading for
Glasgow when first was hit by bombs from a German
aircraft which caused fires, then two days later while
struggling to get to the port she was torpedoed by a German
submarine thus ending the fight to keep it afloat.

Peggy sent a letter thanking me for the photo and I
responded immediately – letters were normally received the
morning after despatch, with several collections from the
pillar boxes and two deliveries each day. German planes
were still raiding London but their bombers now only
attacked at night, a sure indication that their air force could
not gain superiority over our fighters and Hitler's invasion
plan did not materialise. Nevertheless our country still stood
alone in the fight against the Germans, now just 21 miles

away across the Channel. It was cold, wet and windy on Saturday, 2nd November but my day became bright when I received a letter from Mr Davey, he now had my medical report and wished to see me on Monday; Basil called on me as he had a received a similar letter and the news made us quite excited, so we celebrated by going to the Academy and saw Leslie Banks and Lilli Palmer in *"The Door with the Seven Locks"* a gruesome film version of the book by Edgar Wallace. On Monday evening I met up with Basil to fulfil our appointment with Mr Davey; once again it was a pleasing result, we both passed the medical test and were now on course to get our marching orders within a few weeks. He told us we would be advised by telegram when to give a week's notice to our employers and details of the travel arrangements would arrive in the post, then with a handshake and his good wishes it was up to us to follow instructions without even knowing, at this stage, our destination.

Meanwhile I had to try and carry on as normal although the anticipation was always at the back of my mind. On Thursday evening, 7th November, I received a surprise call by Sgt. Garrett, he brought the good news that the night's guard duty had been cancelled and there was a pay parade the next day. At the drill hall in Queen Square I received the princely sum of nineteen shillings and six pence, more importantly we were told that the guard duties were being reviewed and we would be advised of our next duty. I walked back to Freshfield Road with Sgt. Garrett and I gathered from our conversation that the section's activity was being revised because the threat of invasion had subsided; I took this opportunity to tell him of my proposed departure on the farming scheme and said I would be letting him know when I received the notice.

November 11th still remained Armistice Day for the first world war of 1914-1918 and was remembered as usual by the sale of poppy emblems although the two minutes silence was not observed. I helped Gwen Hardy, an old school friend, from my last class at the Junior School in 1933, sell poppies in aid of the British Legion. It seemed strange while in the midst of another war but it was a reminder of what had gone on before which was a recent enough time for our parents to have been greatly affected by the conflict. My father had served in France with the Royal

Garrison Artillery at that time, so was a living part of the history which I learned at school.

Ken's father in uniform 1918

Sgt Garrett called on Tuesday to give me notice that the section was detailed for guard duty next day and to meet at the Golf House; he must have a busy time calling on all the men to round them up for there was no other method of communication. We all felt bound to follow orders so everyone was present when we were transported to Balsdean Pumping Station.

Balsdean Pumping Station

There was a full moon and we had been in this area at the rifle range a month earlier so the landscape was not entirely unfamiliar, although this time we did not branch off but followed the road down into the valley where the tall 1930s structure was dwarfed by the surrounding hills. If there had been a tour of the building prior to setting up the guard I may have been more enthusiastic when walking around in the dead of night, as it was there was a wooden hut which we used as a guard room while taking turns to patrol the area until transport arrived at 5am to take us back to the Golf House. There were several of these water pumping stations in and around the town which were supplying the reservoirs from natural resources deep underground, and I suppose all of them were receiving similar attention from the Home Guard.

I received another letter from Mr Davey which was disappointing as I was expecting marching orders but this was just information about private farm training, such as agricultural colleges, and I never had any intention of making it a career. My meeting with Gwen on Monday must have brought her more to my attention because I particularly noted she was at the Badminton club night on Thursday, but any pleasurable thoughts were quickly overtaken next morning by the shocking news of a heavy air raid on Coventry during the night, in which several hundred German planes indiscriminately dropped bombs and caused considerable causalities amid fires and destruction of buildings including the city's cathedral. No doubt the fact that Coventry was also an industrial centre had much to do with the raid, nevertheless this change of tactics by our enemy was ominous.

I dropped a hint at work about my pending departure and explained about the farming scheme so that my notice of leaving would not come as a complete surprise. In the evening I was again on guard duty, another all night session at Balsdean pumping station, and there was a story reading evening at the youth club on Wednesday after which I walked home with Gwen. We had some games of badminton together on the following evening when I again noted she was very sweet but nothing else, for Peggy was now regarded as my number one girl and the infatuation experienced with Audrey earlier in the year had given me a salutary lesson.

The very next day, Friday 22nd November turned out to be momentous with the arrival of a telegram from the YMCA representative at Derby informing me to give my employer a week's notice and further details would follow; I ascertained that Basil had received a similar message and spent the rest of the evening compiling a letter to Peggy. Naturally I was both excited and apprehensive when handing in my notice to Ronuk on Saturday morning, not yet knowing what the next move would be with only a week to go. In the afternoon I met Jonah and related the events while we were busy cleaning the church brass, there was plenty of it to clean - crosses, candlesticks, flower vases, plaques and the lectern. After tea I put on my Home Guard uniform and reported for duty at the Golf House where our section was unexpectedly detailed to stand guard, very much better than going to Balsdean for I was able to pass the time playing darts and did just one patrol from 12.30 am to 2.45am I arrived home at 5am, well satisfied for I had taken the telegram with me to show Sgt Garrett and he made a note in his pocket book and said "I'll be in touch." In my heart I knew this would turn out to be my last duty with the Home Guard.

By the end of Sunday all my friends at the church knew I would soon be departing; after early morning communion service with Cyril and Owen we met up with Jonah and Frank and the five of us went for a walk about town finishing up in Lyons tea rooms; there were several in Brighton and not all that far apart so we were spoilt for choice. I'm sure this visit to the one in North Street close to the town's biggest and best department store, Hanningtons, was made on the spur of the moment for we did not normally go to these tea rooms. Lyons was renowned for its Nippies, the waitresses who provided a table service and were dressed in the style of French maids; it is inconceivable that we would have been drinking tea at that time of the morning so perhaps we had a milk shake or a mineral. The view from the tea room window narrowly missed looking straight down New Road to the Theatre Royal My only memory of going to the theatre was in my juvenile days when my parents took me to the Christmas pantomimes, it was a story book picture with an interior scrolled like sugar icing, plush red velvet furnishings and subdued lighting; looking up, the three tiers above the stalls seemed to rise into space and I knew the top one was called the Gods, maybe because it was nearer to heaven. Although very old and sandwiched between others, the building is improved by a colonnade along the pavement at that section of New

Road, and is in an ideal position facing the Royal Pavilion gardens.

However, back in the tea room we certainly enjoyed the attention given us by a Nippy and it made a change from sitting on a stool at a milk bar. Our route home took us past Hanningtons, Castle Square and the Old Steine where the town's 1914-18 war Memorial is situated. It was unveiled in the year I was born, 1922, and looks like a Roman structure, with a pool in front which has a small water spray in the centre. There are two square bronze columns, one either side of the white pillars, and these bear the names of well over two thousand men who died in combat. As we passed by there were some poppy wreaths adorning the base of the monument, these had been laid there during the ceremony which had taken place a fortnight earlier on Remembrance Sunday.

The 1914-1918 War Memorial

The War Memorial took all our attention away from the other side of the road where an imposing three tier fountain had been erected long before in 1846. It seems in Queen Victoria's reign there was a plethora of monuments erected both during and after her time 1837-1901 and this was one of them, named the Victoria Fountain which presented an attractive feature in the summer months when it was flood lit. Water spouting from the pinnacle made the top bowl overflow around the rim into the middle bowl which overflowed into the base, this in turn had fine water jets all around the rim and encircled three large cast iron dolphins supporting the bowls above. Flower beds bedecked the area and coloured lights hung in the surrounding trees making it a popular spot for tourists whose cars and coaches would pass this on the way to the seafront and Palace Pier entrance which can be seen a few yards away. However that was over a year ago and the war had changed the scene to one of bleakness but we had adapted to the situation and no longer gave it a thought.

The Victoria Fountain

    A game of golf at Roedean in the afternoon with Jonah and Frank was my last foreseeable visit and the forthcoming week would no doubt bring the "last time" of many activities, a pity Cyril and Owen did not take part because of other commitments but there were still seven days left.

    My last week at Ronuk started with a little tinge of regret at the thought at leaving the familiar faces and surroundings which had been my life for well over three years, but I had made the decision and there was no going back. At the end of the day I opened the anticipated letter from Mr Greenwood the field secretary of the YMCA's farming scheme who operated from Uttoxeter New Road, Derby; this contained a railway voucher with detail of the trains to Derby Station where he would meet me and also Basil on the 3rd December.

On Tuesday evening I went to the Drill Hall with Sgt Garrett to hand in my Home Guard kit including the rifle with five rounds of ammunition; those six months of service could have been a dream for I apparently left without any documentation and no knowledge of which unit I served in, it was my diaries and memories which brought that time to reality. Our youth club meeting on Wednesday had a memorable session on my last attendance by holding a mock trial, a light hearted parody in which I was the Clerk of the Court, and my attempt to keep order turned it into a hilarious evening.

My parents surprised me on Thursday by giving me a wrist watch, I could easily have cried at the thought which lay behind this action for they were already funding me by promising to pay £7.50 to the YMCA, it had not crossed my mind that they would give me a parting present and would miss me. Then I went to the evening's badminton session which was yet another last time activity, Gwen was again mentioned and also a girl, Joan Harrison, who I took home. Joan is just an intriguing pencilled reference in my diary and a signature in my autograph album, but in contrast Gwen contributed by writing

"All good girls love their brothers but I so good have grown,
That I love others brothers better than my own"

and she even included a small photograph so I am unlikely to forget her. The next morning, Friday, 29th November 1940, it dawned on me that this was the last day of my routine for getting to the Ronuk factory by 8.30. But once I had passed the time-office entrance there was no resemblance of normal work due to constant interruptions by well-wishers, including a summons to the Secretary's office, where Crescens Robinsons took his time telling me how sorry he was at my departure and asking me to write with my farm address so they could send me a proposed gift from the staff. At the end of the day I stayed in the time office while the factory girls clocked off as I did not want to leave without seeing some of them, thereby obtaining many goodbye kisses before finally turning my back on the past and making my way to Portslade station.

I had taken my autograph album to work and gathered a few mementos of the day which took the form of signatures, a cartoon by the advertising manager Mr Achard and two versed entries. The one I liked the most was written by Elsie Pearcey who wrote

> *"God gave all men all the earth to love,*
> *But since our hearts are small*
> *Ordains for each, one spot*
> *Should prove beloved over all."*

She worked along with me in the ledger room; we were good pals without romance, so with a promise to write I noted her address at 54 Old Shoreham Road, Portslade. The album had been given to me as a Christmas present in 1932 when it was immediately endorsed by the family, my school class friends signed a page a year later and it also bears the signatures of my friends at St Luke's but little else and strangely does not contain anything by Cyril.

Hannington's, Castle Square, bombed 29th November 1940

In the evening I met Cyril, Jonah and Basil and we went to Normans' milk-shake bar in Duke Street; while there we suddenly heard a loud thump which prompted us to look outside and in the street an incendiary bomb was just starting up like a large firework. We picked up a couple of sandbags and plonked these on top and then went on towards Castle Square. The area was a mass of broken glass crunching under our feet and in the dim light of the new moon it was possible to see that Hannington's was badly damaged and the ARP were already on the scene, so we did not linger but walked on to the Old Steine passing Lindsey's truss makers' shop where we saw a leg hanging out of a shattered window and were relieved to find it was part of their display, although it seemed quite real in the darkness. I arrived home at 10.30 pm to end what had been an extraordinary and unforgettable day.

Sunday, 1st December 1940 was the day for bidding farewell to the church and my friends. I attended the early communion service with my parents at 8.30 and served along with Jonah at the later service, then in the afternoon at 3 o'clock there was a good gathering in the church for a confirmation service and I noted that Gwen Hardy was among those confirmed by the Bishop of Lewes. On each occasion I came away with handshakes, good wishes and even some hugs but there was still the evening to come and I made arrangements to meet Cyril, Jonah, Frank and Basil at the Pepperbox when we went into town. In no particular order we called at the Eight Bells Inn and Chatfields Blue Room which we considered to be upmarket drinking establishments in West Street; at some time we fitted in Norman's milk bar although milkshakes and beer are an unlikely mixture of drinks. It was a very jolly evening in good company and I returned home with a happy frame of mind that everything was going well. The next day I spent the morning visiting relatives before going to the station with Basil to get our tickets for Derby, returning home I packed my camp kitbag and a small case. Included in my kit was a pair of boots and army puttees, thick khaki shirts, thick serge trousers, an ex-post office overcoat and a "hunting, shooting and fishing" hat. I was certainly going prepared; bearing in mind it was the winter season.

After a good night's sleep I was up at seven which gave me an hour to have breakfast, get ready to leave and say good bye to my parents, not forgetting the cat Tinker. As I reached the top of Dawson Terrace, I paused to look back and wave to them before turning the corner out of their sight. I was tinged with sorrow at leaving them but thrilled and apprehensive at what lay ahead. It was an adventure just to go to London yet alone the main lines beyond with their large steam trains, besides which there was a war on and this added to the thrill. With the kitbag on my shoulder I walked along Queens Park Terrace to the Pepperbox where I had arranged to meet Basil, also Jonah for he was coming to the station to see us off and he proved a great help with the luggage. We were soon on a bus and in plenty of time for the 8.56 train to Victoria. Before boarding the train I shook Jonah's hand and thanked him for being such a good friend over the years, then waved to him as the train left the platform to take Basil and me to an unknown destination and future.

We duly arrived in Victoria station at 10.30 and not wanting to get into difficulties finding our own way across London we took a taxi which reached St Pancras a mere fifteen minutes later. Following Mr Greenwood's instructions this gave us plenty of time to catch the midday train which brought us into Derby station at 4.15 pm It seemed a long journey and I was apparently too intent on getting there to assimilate all the sights and sounds experienced while on the way, also to appreciate that the trains we caught were running near to normal in spite of the recent and continuing heavy bombing raids. Mr Greenwood was waiting to meet us when the train came to a stop, he could hardly miss two youngsters burdened down with luggage stepping on to the platform, and he quickly made himself known and helped us to his car

As he drove slowly along the country roads I had no idea where we were for by now it was dark, the vehicle's lights were masked in accordance with the blackout regulations and I knew the signposts had been removed although I could never have seen them in this moonless night. Basil was the first to be left at a farm, I never saw him again but did hear later that he didn't stay to complete the course, so perhaps it was just as well we were not together at the same place. Mr Greenwood continued on to my placement which we reached at 6pm and he introduced me to Tom Spencer the farmer or the "Gaffer" as he was called.

December 1940 to June 1941

Life on the Farm

My arrival at Alton Manor Farm had been expected and Tom Spencer led me into the farmhouse parlour to meet his wife and young daughter June, then almost immediately he lit a hurricane lamp and invited me to accompany him on a tour of the farm buildings, but I could not see them very well because of the dim light. When we returned to the farmhouse I was surprised to meet another youngster, Dick Lewis, who was an ex-YMCA trainee and a resident retained by the Gaffer so I was not alone. Supper was a communal affair around a huge table, lit by an ornate oil lamp with a glass reservoir supplying two wicks which burnt brightly under a large glass globe. I was able to get a better impression of my new acquaintances as we ate and talked over the meal. I guessed the Gaffer was in his 40s, weather beaten and sprightly with a sense of humour, his wife was homely and obviously very capable at running the household, I always addressed her as the "Mrs". Their daughter, June, appeared to be a well behaved sweetie, and Dick Lewis had an easy going attitude with conversation. I was very much at ease with the company around the table which was a good start, so when we retired early carrying candles and hot water bottles I lost no time in falling asleep in the comfortable bed.

The next thing I knew was being aroused by the Gaffer at 5.30am, it was rather like being roused for a guard duty so the early time did not affect me. I got up, put on my working gear, dabbed my face with water from a hand basin and joined the others in the cow shed. I thought I knew how to milk a cow because I had given it a try at Church Farm but soon realised the difference between a few minutes of holiday fun and the serious business of milking as a job. It was a struggle to cope with the strange situation that I suddenly found myself in. Sitting on a three legged stool with a bucket between my knees and my head resting on the beast's flank, milking by the dim light of hurricane lamps on a cold winter morning amid the smell and the mess made by the animals, all very different from the warm office environment I had left behind. Although I had been given the easiest cows to milk I only managed three during the time the Gaffer, Dick and another farmhand named Arthur, finished milking the rest of the herd which totalled fifty

The milk was poured from the buckets through a filter into churns which held seventeen gallons; inside each one, near the top, were graduation marks which indicated the number of gallons in the churn up to its full capacity. These churns were quite tall and tapered with a handle both side and it was an art to move them, especially when full, for they had to be tipped forward then rolled on the rim round the base by twisting the top like a steering wheel. The milking had to be completed and the churns made ready in time for collection by the milk lorry; it took two persons to lift them on to the back of the vehicle which was three to four foot off the ground and I did not attempt to help with this until I became more familiar with the procedure.

Our next job was to clean out the cowshed pushing a barrow to a special compound where what we had removed would later be used to fertilize the fields. Then the cows were fed with a recipe comprising – 2 bags chopped straw, 20 baskets brewers grains, 2 tubs ground oats, 1 tub premier dairy meal and 1 barrow load of chopped swedes. This was all thoroughly mixed together and more or less distributed in equal portions to the cows. By this time it would be roughly 8.30 and we would go into the house for breakfast.

I found the meals prepared by Mrs S. were really good; there was nothing I disliked although it took a little while getting used to eating the sweet before the main course which was the custom in this part of the country. The main meal was taken at midday and my first experience was to be given a dish of rice pudding, thinking this was all there would be I readily accepted a second helping and was more than surprised to be served next with meat and vegetables. However the "when in Rome" proverb stood me in good stead and I became used to the reversed order of the meal. Fortunately, food did not seem a problem despite the war. Milk and cream were plentiful and used to make butter and cheese, chickens roamed about the farm providing free range eggs and the occasional table bird. Wild rabbits were fairly abundant and the odd wood pigeon, water fowl or even a pheasant made a change of fare. Fruit and vegetables including mushrooms were within a stone's throw of the farmhouse according to the season, and extra rations for farm workers also helped. Then there was bacon, not just a rasher but a whole pig which was killed just before Christmas; boiling water was poured over the carcass and the bristles were scraped off with broken glass before being cut into pieces and preserved in salt, nothing was wasted.

The cows were fed again at 15.30 with oats and hay, and then there was tea break before commencing the afternoon's milking. My fingers ached from the unaccustomed use of muscles, it was painful and I was very unhappy. The weather did not help because it was cold and wet with ice and snow. In addition to the cows, the Gaffer had many other animals, calves, steers, heifers, sheep and horses. Milking the cows and looking after all this stock was the daily routine and in between times there were numerous other jobs to be done. The farm was located just off a narrow country road (B5023) roughly half way between a small village, Idridgehay, and a market town, Wirksworth. On my first Saturday evening, 7th December, I walked with Dick to Wirksworth a distance of about one and a half miles. We visited the only cinema and saw the film "*Destry Rides Again*" then afterwards we bought some fish and chips, eating them on the walk back to the farmhouse. This outing set a pattern and we went to the Wirksworth cinema often, watching films like "*Dodge City*" and Deanna Durbin in "*First Love*". I may previously have seen them in Brighton for the bigger cinemas got the new films first, but it was the evening out that mattered.

A week after arriving at the farm I received my first letter from my mother which added to my home sickness. I shed many tears feeling very much alone and upset but endeavoured to hide my depression from the others because I was determined to stick it out. I wrote a long letter in reply pouring my heart out to them telling them about the work and my hope of getting home for Christmas. The next day, 12th December, I tackled the Gaffer about going home for those two special days and he said I would have to get approval from the YMCA. I wrote to Mr Greenwood and he was not keen on my going, pointing out that my sponsors would not like to think they were helping me with my training while I could afford the fare to go home. I made out that my parents were paying the fare and he reluctantly agreed. The knowledge that I would be spending Christmas at home enabled me to overcome this difficult period. I tried to regularly attend the church at Idridgehay, it was in such a lovely peaceful setting, but after the second Sunday I had to give up as it was so much of a rush to make myself look respectable and walk there in time for the morning service at eleven o'clock. Mrs S. was extremely good in delaying the dinner; nevertheless I felt this was not fair on the family.

The church at Idridgehay

On the 16th December, I received a postal package from Ronuk which contained my leaving present: a Swan fountain pen and a Morden propelling pencil. I thought them a handsome gift and the pen was instantly used in writing a letter of thanks, then with constant use it became indispensable. Three days later I cycled to Idridgehay and ascertained the times of the bus and train in readiness for the journey home on the 24th; I also found out the cost of the return rail fare from Derby to Brighton which was one pound sixteen shillings and nine pence (£1.16s.9d).

I was much happier with the anticipation of Christmas at home and the days seemed to pass quickly. In addition to the milking we were kept busy in the fields mainly muck spreading and digging up cabbage stalks. The former was no easy task first having to cart the dung from the compound to the fields, and then spread it over the land with a dung fork, this had six prongs and a fork full of dung was given a twist causing it to break up in the air and spread over the ground. When I first tried this I showered it over myself! The evenings were mostly spent in the cosy farm parlour writing, reading and sometimes playing draughts or cards. I sent and received a large number of letters during this time not only between my long standing friends but also with colleagues and acquaintances for whom my absence from Brighton was fresh in the memory. There were some surprising correspondents like the ex-girl friend from earlier in the year Audrey Lloyd, who along with her family sent me a Christmas present, forwarded by my parents. I had not seen her since she moved to Farnham the previous July.

When the morning of the 24th arrived I was up at six which was a bit later than usual. Mrs S. was most thoughtful in packing me a piece of salted pork and some rations to take home. I set off on the 7.40 Trent bus to Derby and caught the 9.07 LMS train which reached St Pancras at 1.15pm. For the first time I was by myself in London and with the aid of a pocket map I walked across the city to Victoria station, gazing spellbound at the scene which was too much for me to assimilate as I passed by Oxford Street, Marble Arch, Park Lane and Hyde Park Corner. The 3.28pm from Victoria got me to Brighton at 5. It was lovely being back home with my parents, and I did not have long to wait before my friends Cyril, Jonah and Frank joined me for the evening.

I seemed to spend most of the morning on Christmas Day attending church for Holy Communion services, at 8.00 with my sister, at 9.00 serving with Jonah and at 11.00 serving with my father. Cyril, Jonah and Frank called on me in the evening and we played Monopoly, visited the Beaufort, played cards back at home and just sat around the fireside talking until 3am, even then I do not think we really wanted to part company. It was astonishing to note that I met Gwen Hardy on Boxing Day morning at 10.30, a date arranged twenty four hours earlier at the church. We walked the full extent of the racecourse, down the valley through the golf links to Ovingdean and back along the seafront, a walk taking two and a half hours so she must have liked me, more so because we met again later, this time with the company of an ex girl friend, Joan Gilmore. The three of us visited the Astoria cinema and watched the film "*Dancing on a Dime*". It was a good show and very pleasing to be sitting between the two girls and walking back afterwards to the

Pepperbox before parting at 7.30. I then called on Jonah and we rounded up Cyril and Frank for a good wishes drink in the Beaufort.

"*Fare thee well Home sweet Home*" was an appropriate entry in the diary on the 27th when the short holiday was over. Jonah came to the station with me and saw me away on the 8.56 to Victoria, this time I caught a bus to St Pancras and was back in Derby at 3.30pm. My first action was to phone the YMCA to let Mr Greenwood know that I had not deserted, and also with a thought he might give me a lift. However he was out so I caught a bus which arrived at the farm in time for tea. Mrs S. greeted me like a son; she was sweet and had bought me two handkerchiefs. The very next morning I was up early, milking the cows with little difficulty and feeling surprisingly cheerful. I was becoming accustomed to my surroundings; the pang of missing my parents and friends was losing its intensity. A few days later, on New Years Eve, I was with the Gaffer to help at the birth of a calf and this new experience for me did not seem a bad way of ending 1940. The country was at war and we certainly did not bother to usher in the New Year. I guess we lit the candles, filled the hot water bottles and went upstairs to bed at the usual time of 9.30.

The start of 1941, and my new Collins Farmers Diary inscribed "*From Cyril with best wishes for the future*" was a thoughtful present from him and one I would treasure. There were 130 pages covering all aspects of farming from animals to crops, measurements and calculations even to estimating the contents of a haystack. A random glance under the heading "Milk, Butter & Cheese" urges that the udder of each cow be wiped with a damp cloth before milking, that the first two streams of milk from each teat be discarded into a separate vessel, and that no operation of feeding or cleaning be performed simultaneously with or prior to milking, which is precisely what we did.

Alton Manor Farm derived its name from the Manor which was a large stone building a short walk across the fields. The Gaffer supplied the Big House, as it was called, with produce and I often went there with Mrs S delivering milk and eggs, but we were never invited beyond the kitchen. There was a lake nearby aptly referred to as the Manor Lake although I thought it to be more like a large pond. On Sunday, 5th January, I noted that while taking a stroll around the farm I was able to walk across the lake as it was frozen over with thick ice, and I wondered where the water hens had gone because they made a nice meal. Two days later, when I was half way through my training course, Dick Lewis received some service papers from the RAF and would probably be called up, I knew I would miss him if he left the farm before me as we spent a lot of time together. On the following day all of us were worried when two cows became sick. They were frothing at the mouth and very dopey, so the Gaffer called in the vet who found nothing seriously wrong and put the trouble down to them having eaten frosted cabbage or grass.

Throughout January it snowed a great deal and lay very thick, but the milking, mucking out and feeding the stock went on just the same, however, it was not possible to work on the fields so I was given the task of hedging, along with an experienced hand named Ted. This was just the right time of the year to trim and lay the hedgerows, while there was no foliage on the branches. Armed with billhooks and wearing thick leather gloves, Ted and I moved along a hedgerow trimming it down to a uniform height, often it was necessary to partly cut through a branch or sapling and bend it horizontal, then weave it among the other branches where it would continue to grow, thereby closing gaps and thickening the hedge. I took my cue from Ted and liked the job, especially as we burnt the cuttings in the field while we worked our way along a hedge, and the smell of the wood smoke reminded me of camp fires during past times at Spithurst.

Although it was the winter season the countryside around the farm was really beautiful. There were undulating fields of pasture, dotted here and there with a spinney or copse which harboured many a pheasant and rabbit, more like the park of a large estate. It was a pleasant walk over the fields to reach the village of Kirk Ireton and I went there on several occasions with the Gaffer and Dick for a drink in the village pub. Whenever I had the chance I would wander to a five barred gate near the farmhouse and gaze upon the sloping ground towards the horizon; watching the dawn of a new day and being entranced by the stillness of the surroundings, the haze over the fields, and the rising sun bringing light to the sky. The scene always brought peace to my mind and became a panacea for the home sickness which still beset me at times.

Snow in January tempted Dick and me to knock together a sledge and we spent an hour or so one Sunday sliding like a couple of schoolboys, although we had the excuse it was for the amusement of the Gaffer's daughter, June. Thus there were pleasant moments between those when I was cursing the cold white flakes which made working on the farm so uncomfortable. Also during the lull on Sundays, the Gaffer, Dick and I with one or two others often went ferreting for rabbits. Carrying shotguns, spades, nets and a ferret or two in a sack, we would make our way to a rabbit warren and stake nets over all the holes we could find.

Ferreting for rabbits on the farm

A ferret would then be put into one of the burrows and within seconds any rabbits underground could be heard going hell for leather to get out of the warren. They usually ended up rushing straight into a net, but sometimes appeared from a hole which had escaped our attention and these were dispatched by a shotgun. It was not always that simple for the ferret might catch up with the rabbit underground, in which case the ferret would not come to the surface with his prey and had to be dug out of the warren.

This could take a long time, excavating the earth along the burrow and endeavouring to ascertain where the ferret was by listening with an ear to the ground; we always got there in the end and came away with a good number rabbits which the Gaffer sold after deducting our dinner.

January 30th was a Thursday and in the evening I went to Wirksworth with Dick to visit the cinema and see the film "*Typhoon*" starring Dorothy Lamour. Our habit was to make this outing on a Saturday but we couldn't wait to see this glamorous sexy film star of the time. On the following day Dick accompanied the Gaffer to the Derby farmers market and I was promised a similar outing the next week. The month ended and my feeling of discontent still lingered but my perseverance prevailed. I was always writing letters as this helped to ease my thoughts and looking back at the 31 days I counted a total of 19 letters being sent and 16 received. One in particular had arrived four days ago on the 28th from my steady girl friend Peggy; she was honest in telling me that someone else had taken my place, I should have realised it was an awkward letter to write but it was just like her to do the right thing. I was upset with this coming on top of the struggle with farming and much to my shame appear have ignored the letter, and also her birthday on the 26th February so our affection which had blossomed on and off since 1937 had come to an end.

There were now just eleven more days to pass before reaching the end of my ten weeks' training, the first week in February seemed to pass quickly and this was likely due to an improvement in the weather. The snow had begun to thaw and it was possible to resume work in the fields, lifting cabbage stalks, muck spreading, clearing ditches and hedging. I was also now quite accustomed to the horses and had learned how to fit their harness for attachment to the carts or machines. Horses were very common on the farms and it was part of the job to know how to handle them, and also the appliances they pulled.

As promised, the Gaffer took me to Derby in his car on the 7th February, but there was no market owing to an outbreak of foot and mouth disease. We returned to the farm early in the afternoon and although the trip made a change for me I was bitterly disappointed at not having seen the market in operation. Twenty four hours later I was helping with the birth of a calf for the second time, it was so satisfying watching the mother lick her new born clean before it shakily stood up to suckle. The Gaffer then introduced Dick and I to a new farm hand, John Rowlands, we both took an instant liking to him but time at the farm was running out for both of us.

My ten week training period expired on the 11th February; there was no word from the YMCA and the Gaffer said he would pay me until Mr Greenwood brought advice of my next job. I spent the evening in the pub at Kirk Ireton, playing darts with Dick and John which was, to say the least, somewhat different from the following evening when the three of us trooped down the road to the Idridgehay church hall for a whist drive. Arriving at our destination I realised that my hunting, shooting and fishing hat made me look a proper country yokel or Right Charlie. No one took any notice of my appearance and neither did anyone get upset at the mistakes I made when playing the cards, in fact it was a very jovial evening, rounded off by a drink in the nearby Black Swan Inn before returning to the farm.

Gradually the days passed and I became more apprehensive at the absence of Mr Greenwood but he eventually arrived a week late on the 18th February. Events then moved fast for he had arranged to take me to meet a Mr Hutchinson, the Gaffer of Thulston Fields Farm near Derby, on the following day. I duly met Mr Hutchinson and he must have liked my face for he offered me a job and it was agreed that I take up residence at the farm on the 25th, which would allow me to have a few days at home. Returning to Alton Manor farm I immediately set about packing my kitbag. Mrs S cooked me a special breakfast the next morning. She also gave me another piece of salted pork to take home, and along with the others seemed to be genuinely sorry to see me leave. As I set off for Derby my mind was a whirl of mixed feelings. I had no qualms about the new job for I was now familiar with the farm environment and fairly efficient at milking, rolling churns, humping sacks, handling livestock and horses, hedging, ditching, twisting the muck fork or just shovelling. I felt fit, strong, confident and above all no longer homesick and not unhappy at the thought of returning to work at Thulston Fields. The Gaffer and Mrs S were, perhaps unknowingly, largely to thank for this change in my attitude and outlook to life, which was to stand me in good stead in future years. Even so, I was already intent on joining the RAF as soon as I was able and therefore did not regard my prospects at Thulston Fields with any thought of permanency. I took one last wistful look at the hundreds of snowdrops which were now in flower along the drive leading to the farmhouse; the scene was imprinted in my memory as were the eleven weeks I had spent with the Gaffer (Tom) and Mrs S for in that short time they had given me so much.

The four whole days back in Brighton simply flew by, meeting up with my friends who played such a large part in my life, we met mainly in the evenings, except on the Sunday (23rd) when we were at the Church and Dick (Whittington) was also able to join us as he was home on leave. I visited the Ronuk office to see my old colleagues and was given a good reception, and of course I spent a lot of time with my parents, helping them on the last day by restoring the chicken runs in the back garden. Jonah yet again saw me off from the station on Tuesday (25th) when I returned to Derby using the same timetable as I did at Christmas. As arranged Mr Hutchinson, my new Gaffer met me at the station and we drove to Thulston Fields Farm.

Any apprehensions I had were immediately dispelled when we reached the farmhouse within thirty minutes and I was introduced to Mrs H who showed me a common room for the employees and then upstairs to my bedroom, these two rooms and a back kitchen were seemingly set apart from those occupied by the Hutchinsons an arrangement which worked very well. He then took me around the farm buildings which were more extensive than Alton Manor as it was a much larger farm with a lot more cows, heifers and steers; returning to the house I had a meal in the common room along with two new companions Jim and Rose. Jim, who also lived in, was the son of a farmer at Bakewell and was unable to work for his father as there was control over the employment of farmhands due to their exemption from the armed forces, possibly his father knew the Gaffer who was able to help by taking him on the payroll. Naturally I took more interest in Rose and was destined to get to know her well, she was employed to give general help to Mrs H. in the house, and lived in Thulston Village although sometimes stayed overnight at the farm.

I soon became accustomed to my new habitat which was only about four miles along the A6 from Derby. This main road passes through Alvaston before reaching Thulston, a small village at the head of a minor road leading to Elvaston and Burrowash; close by this junction, on the opposite side of the A6, another lane leads to the farm and on to Chellaston. It was an easy walk to Thulston but a longer walk to Alvaston where local buses went to Derby. The surrounding land was flat, the farm stood out amidst the fields and I felt happy about living here for the next few months. I was also able to attend the nearest church at Elvaston every Sunday at 11.00. My stroll to this attractive stone building gave me much pleasure for just across the A6 a long avenue ended at the locked gated western entrance to a large mansion and a path to the church, when traversing the avenue it was fascinating to watch the dozens of squirrels who had built their drays in the trees.

My first day commenced at 6am and I was put to work in the dairy which entailed collecting the buckets of milk from those whose job it was to milk the cows, then pouring it through the cooler into 17 gallon churns. The cooler was similar to a very large washboard made of stainless steel, like all the utensils, it was hollow to contain cold water and had a large tank on the top into which I emptied the buckets; this enabled the milk to flow evenly down the corrugations and through a filter into a churn. This kept me busy until all the cows were milked, which filled several churns, and then I had the laborious work of cleaning the equipment before sterilizing it in a steam cabinet. Meanwhile the others were hard at it mucking out the cowsheds and feeding the animals. This procedure was repeated in the afternoon at 4 o'clock and became routine for me with few exceptions, I was pleased not to be milking the cows. The work between milking times was much more varied than at Alton Manor as many fields were cultivated and there were at least four men employed as well as Jim and me. During the first week I spent some time with Jim cutting kale in one of the fields, this was one of the ingredients given to the cattle but I took little part in actually feeding the dairy herd. On the Saturday I went to the Rex Cinema in Alvaston with Jim and upon coming out at 9.30 we lost our way in the pitch black night and did not get back to the farm until midnight. I made my first visit to the Church the next day and in the evening explored the pub at Thulston.

It was my father's birthday on Thursday, 6th March and I went to the pub again to drink his health, but not before an interesting variation to the working day helping with the threshing. The thresher which was like a huge rectangular box on wheels arrived at the farm pulled by a steam engine and stopped alongside a large barn which was full of wheat from the previous year's harvest. The engine was coupled to the thresher by a long drive belt while we prepared the empty sacks and erected a small mesh fence around the area of the barn, and when all was ready the driver tooted his steam whistle and started the fly wheel to turn the drive belt and bring to life the threshing machine. There were two of us on top of the wheat stack with pitch forks feeding the sheaves into the top of the thresher, two on the ground at one side where the grain came out of a spout filling the sacks, and two on the other side where the chaff was being ejected. A youngster, helped by a cat, was enthusiastically disposing of the mice which ran out of the stack and were trapped by the mesh fence. I had no idea how the mechanism in the thresher worked and all the activity coupled with the noise and dust must have appeared to be pretty chaotic but it did the job to produce sacks of grain. The steam engine and thresher did not leave until late on Monday so it had taken nearly four working days to process the stored harvest into grain for the cattle. On the following Thursday I visited the Thulston pub to drink my mother's health for it was her birthday, exactly a week after my father's and they were both born in the same year 1884; it was pleasing to have the company of John who was one of the farmhands and I went back to his house which was No. 11 Thulston, before returning to the farm.

A letter and newspaper from home arrived on Saturday 15th which contained the worrying news of an air raid on the Tuesday night when bombs fell near our house in Dawson Terrace. My mother wrote of her experience and fortunately the damage to the property was superficial, roof tiles blown off and a few windows broken, it was the dust and soot being sucked down the chimneys which took much time and effort cleaning up. The local newspaper, *The Evening Argus,* dated 12th March 1941, contained a picture of my sister in the back garden by our air raid shelter; she was holding my niece Wendy who was three years old. The caption of the picture read "*The bomb fell a few yards away ... This home-made shelter, built into the garden remained intact although debris was flung hundreds of yards from a bomb crater in a nearby garden during a recent raid at a South Coast Town*". The front page of the Argus carried a more detailed report with a large picture of the bomb damage at the rear of No. 5 Dawson Terrace (this address was omitted) with a 12ft crater in the garden, just four houses away from ours, the householder Mr Ernest Burnet-Smith was killed and his wife Laura was injured. It was a relief to learn my parents had come to no harm and I thought the reference to our air raid shelter was ironical for it was never used by them. They later had a Morrison steel shelter erected in the dining room and this made a functional table which they could crawl under during an air raid and was reasonably comfortable.

On the next day, Sunday, I missed going to church and caught the bus to Derby, the first of many such visits and this one was specifically to meet up with Dick Lewis from Alton Manor Farm. We had lunch and a walk around town but parted company early as we had to get back for the afternoon milking sessions. At the farmhouse I had noticed a couple of shotguns in a cloak cupboard but did not like to approach the Gaffer about using one on the farm, until the opportunity arose one evening during the week when there was some discussion about a meal for the next day and I suggested shooting a rabbit. The Gaffer was surprisingly agreeable and offered me the use of his old single barrelled 12 bore; it required a piece of a matchstick to be stuck in the hole where the foresight was missing but otherwise was quite serviceable. He enquired how many cartridges I needed and in a cocksure manner I asked how many rabbits did we want, and when he said one I responded by saying that would be enough. A huge grin came over his face as with the gun and one cartridge I set off confidently along the hedgerows surrounding the fields. I became less sure of myself an hour or so later for no bunnies had presented themselves as a target; it was getting darker by the minute when at last I came to a five barred gate and there, on the other side was a bunny sitting on its haunches. I fired my one shot and the animal jumped into the air and started running away, for a fraction of a second I thought I had missed when it suddenly bowled over. In my excitement I dropped the gun, scrambled over the fence and grabbed the bunny which was well and truly dead, then returning over the fence I had difficulty in finding the gun as the light was so bad. My triumphant return to the farmhouse was greeted with amazement, we ate the rabbit the next day and thereafter I was able to go shooting whenever I liked.

I walked around the fields with the gun exactly a week after my lucky shot and bagged another rabbit especially to send home, so I gutted it ready for the next day and then made a parcel which I posted to Brighton. There were many such occasions when I roamed the fields with the gun, usually in the evening after work when all was quiet and the day was ending which is a good time for seeing rabbits nibbling the vegetation before the sun had set. The fact that I was able to do this was a real bonus and I felt privileged the Gaffer had shown his trust in me within such a short time. In my earlier days camping at Church Farm, where I first became acquainted with guns, the golden rule was never point the barrel at anyone at any time, and this stood me in good stead at the farms although the rule certainly did not apply when I was standing guard over the reservoirs at home. There was no doubt I liked guns, the power of them and the satisfaction of hitting the centre of the target, but I became upset at shooting wild life without good reason. This circumstance happened to me at Thulston when a large wood pigeon took flight from a tree and without a thought I quickly raised the gun and fired. The bird was flying away and my shot hit its rear stripping many feathers which blew back at me like a split pillow case as the pigeon glided down to earth. Upon picking up the dead pigeon it was warm, bald in places where the shot had hit its pristine feathers, and I immediately felt regret at my impulsive action for unlike a rabbit it was insufficient for a meal at the farm. However I walked on to the farm cottage where Ted was pleased to accept it and this made me feel more at ease with myself for thoughtlessly shooting the bird.

Elvaston Church was filled with the congregation on Sunday 23rd for a rousing service as it was the National Day of Prayer and our voices were singing with gusto. During the week which followed I was sent to help at another farm in the vicinity of Alvaston, but did not record the address or the Gaffer's connection with this place. I worked here for a

couple of days on the 25th/26th helping the threshing with
the same steam engine as two weeks back, then there was
an occasion when I collected a mare to bring back to the
farm and also took a cow in the reverse direction. The main
road was devoid of traffic and it was no problem leading a
farm animal a couple of miles along the highway.

Ken muck carting and spreading

April commenced with rain but it was warmer and
there were signs of life in the buds of the country flora also
the birds were becoming frisky. I loved this time of the year
and even the work of muck spreading to fertilise the fields
did not seem so much of a chore, the operation varied
between spreading an area or distributing the manure along
shallow trenches depending on what was to be planted. It
was an important task for without fertilisation the crop
would not flourish. Jim and I took turns to lead the horse
and cart which had to be negotiated through the fields to
and from the muck compound whenever a fresh load was
required. A day's work at this with breaks for lunch and
milking, then parking the cart and attending to the horse in
its stable was certainly not for the faint hearted. Jim took
these photographs of me with his box camera and I was not
to realise at the time how precious they were to become. The
hunting shooting and fishing hat was part of my working
gear along with the khaki shirt, serge trousers, puttees and

boots but I always changed into more respectable clothes when not at work.

The Easter break from Friday 11th to Monday 14th was surprisingly quiet; I was able to catch up with my correspondence for the days were treated as a Sunday with only the milking to do, except for the Saturday when I worked as normal on the land with Ted. This was the last of three days we had spent drilling some land with seeds for a grain crop, it was my job to lead the horse pulling the drilling machine while Ted walked behind attending to its operation. The week after Easter I was singled out for digging the kitchen garden then mowing the lawn, fortunately the mower broke down on Friday so completion of that operation was postponed, and on Saturday I was happily back in the fields with the horse and muck cart which suited me better than mowing a lawn. In the evening I asked Rose out to the cinema and although she refused we went for a walk in the home fields and seemed to get on well together; maybe this was the reason I gave her some violets the next day which I had picked on my way back from the Church. I think the Gaffer liked my company for on the following day he took me with him to Kegworth which was a few miles along the A6; he had some business to do there and invited me to accompany him. I well recall we set off in his new Jaguar car like a rocket along a straight stretch of road and he had to brake fairly hard to stop running into the back of another vehicle, he chuckled and referred to the Jag's acceleration being different to his previous car.

Two days later I went with the Gaffer's wife to visit her parents' grave at Horsley, a small village some twelve miles to the north which we reached by driving along quiet country roads. Upon arrival I was in my element with the lovely old church of St Clement and its graveyard, for some reason I am always enthralled with such places perhaps due to the memory of those at Spithurst and Isfield along with the happy times at Church Farm. These country churches usually provide a fascinating history of the people who lived in the locality hundreds of years ago, and at the time of this visit to Horsley in April 1941 I thought it a haven of tranquillity in contrast to the death and destruction which was taking place in our towns and cities. I suppose I should have considered myself fortunate but the truth was I felt out of the fray and not content with the quiet life the country seemed to provide. This particular outing made a pleasant break from the task of muck spreading which continued throughout the rest of the month except for Tuesday 29th when I was briefly back to mowing the lawn as the mower had been repaired.

I noted on Saturday, 3rd May that the clocks were put forward an hour until August, this being in addition to British Summer Time and was intended to assist farmers by providing more daylight in the evenings. It did not affect me for I was rarely asked to work in the fields beyond my usual job of cleaning the dairy after the second milking session, for by then it would be about five thirty. The extra daylight would no doubt be of great help during the time of haymaking and harvesting but it was my intention to leave before then. There was an interesting event on Sunday afternoon when I was returning from walking to the main road with Rose. My attention was drawn to a flimsy looking biplane which was circling round the farm then it surprisingly levelled out and landed close by in one of our meadows. I quickly reached the plane just as the pilot was getting out of the cockpit, he assured me all was well and some chaps were already on their way to fix something before he could take off. True enough, an RAF truck arrived which was easily able to reach the aircraft, and two hours later the plane took off.

The alteration to the clocks was coincidental to a change in my work pattern as the Gaffer gave me a different task or tasks each day, some were very mundane, such as chopping sticks and spring cleaning the back kitchen, I silently resented being the house boy although this was compensated by the variety of jobs around the farm. My mind was set on the 26th May for then I would be nineteen and able to join the RAF. I was often in Derby where the milk-bars and pubs were crowded with people in uniform mingling with the noise of the jukeboxes, mostly playing records of the Andrews Sisters, Glen Miller and Vera Lynn - visions and sounds which made me feel very much out of things, so much so, that on Sunday, 18th May I posted a letter through their Recruiting Office door to enquire about joining. There was not long to wait as three days later, Wednesday 21st, a reply came asking me to call at the office for an interview on my birthday. I had to show the letter to the Gaffer for it meant having the afternoon off, he expressed surprise at the notice and immediately wanted to get me exempted from the forces so I could continue working at the farm, but I assured him I was happy to join up.

My birthday turned out better than expected, I received cards from my family, Cyril sent one from "The Boys" and there were several from girls who had not yet forgotten me. Peggy's card followed upon a letter in which between the lines there was still a spark of affection, this time I responded but for me there was no thought of rekindling our relationship. In the afternoon I duly kept my appointment at the recruiting office in Derby. It was a bitter disappointment when the sergeant behind the desk ruled out my hope of flying as he noted I wore spectacles, and then he suggested I became a Ground Gunner which was a trade urgently being recruited at the present time. Naïve that I was, the thought of firing guns appealed to me. I filled in the necessary forms, passed a medical exam A1 for that trade and left with instructions to report back at the office next Monday morning for the attestation which would entail an overnight stay at Padgate.

That evening I was surprised when Rose took me to the Blue Peter which my diary suggests was a pub in Alvaston and there we met another girl who was with one of my work mates. The four of us visited several inns, a pub crawl in fact which finished up at the Harrington in Thulston and we were all quite merry by closing time; this must have been prearranged and I was grateful for their company which brought such a pleasurable ending to the day. During the week I was working in the pastures 'knocking and docking', a leisurely job walking around the fields scattering cow pats and uprooting any self seeded docks which were a large weed growing among the grasses. It was the end of May, the cows were now out in the pastures, plants were growing rapidly, and at dusk I walked stealthily along the hedgerows and shot two rabbits.

The month of June commenced with a Sunday and I skipped church to visit the Spencers at Alton Manor Farm which was to be the last time I would set foot on my farm training ground. I had much affection for them and we had a pleasant time over lunch along with my pal Dick Lewis, afterwards we walked over the familiar landscape constantly chatting until about 3 o'clock when they had work to do. The return bus arrived in Derby well in time for me to go the

Regal Cinema and spend an hour playing the pin tables
while listening to haunting tunes from a jukebox, before
making tracks to Thulston Fields where I was early enough
to have a bath ready for the morrow.

The day had come; it was Whit Monday although Bank
Holidays were now like any other day. I worked in the dairy
as usual then changed my clothes, packed an overnight bag
and presented myself at the Derby Recruiting Office by 9.15.
There were eight of us in the party escorted by a Sergeant,
not everyone arrived on time much to his annoyance and we
missed the intended train. It meant a long wait of two hours
before we boarded the 12.09 for the rather tedious rail route
to Manchester and then to Warrington where we had RAF
transport to Padgate, the journey had taken five hours.

Padgate seemed to be a complex of wooden buildings
and we were first shown our sleeping quarters in Hut
No. 189, and then the Mess for a meal before going to the
attestation rooms for the first part of the enrolment
procedure. I recall we sat at separate tables like a class
room and were handed papers containing elementary
questions on maths, geography and general knowledge
which needed to be completed in an hour, a visit to the
NAAFI was then in order. I had a good night in the hut
which had beds down either side and would have held more
than the eight in our group. Each bed had the springs
neatly covered by three palliasses and there were two
blankets, a small bolster pillow but no sheets. Getting
undressed and putting on pyjamas in the company of seven
strangers did not worry me as it was paradise compared to
my Home Guard experience. We were roused early by an
RAF Corporal, had breakfast in the Mess and assembled in
the attestation room at eight o'clock where it took all the
morning to check our details, issue the completed RAFVR
Enlistment Form 2150 which showed my number which was
vitally important and like most servicemen it would remain a
lifetime memory. I also received a railway warrant for the
journey back; then we stood in front of an officer and were
sworn in.

Our photographs were taken, and a reminder given
that we would shortly be called up for permanent service.
Then we were released to have a meal in the Mess and
another visit to the NAAFI before setting off for the railway
station to go our separate ways. My railway warrant would

have taken me home to Brighton which was very tempting, but I could not desert Thulston Fields in that way so travelled via Manchester to Derby arriving in the early evening.

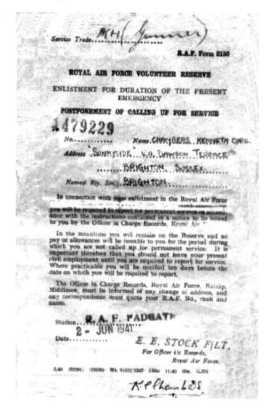

Ken's RAFVR
Enlistment Form
2nd June 1941

It was back to work as usual on Wednesday, 4th June and it was less than three weeks later, on the 23rd when I received a phoned telegram from my father advising the call up notice had arrived for me to report to Blackpool on 4th July. The intervening days including three weekends seemed to pass almost too fast because my social life had become more enjoyable, possibly due to the knowledge my days at Thulston were numbered. My last visit to the church was on Sunday 8th and in the evening I went with the Gaffer in the Jag to Derby, we visited the Regent Arcade, then a pub where he appeared to be well known, and discussed farming matters, before returning. The Gaffer had certainly become more amicable and was quite a sport, so much so that he even had a race with me in the Paddock which I often jogged around for the exercise.

I was spending more time with Rose and was often at No. 19 Thulston were she lived with her parents, also my frequent visits to the village pub, the Harrington Arms, became a favourite spot for a restful break. There was an amusing episode when I happened to be alone in the pub garden one Friday evening sipping a half pint of Burton's. Two mature ladies asked to join me; they had walked from Alvaston and were both weary and thirsty. Badly wanting a drink and knowing nothing about pubs they decided on pints of Burton's and gave me £1.10s to buy them, this sum would have bought buckets full but I returned all their change and finished up walking back with them to Alvaston.

During the last two weekends I went to Derby, on the Saturdays I visited the Gaumont cinema with Jim to see the films "*So Ends our Night*" and "*Inspector Hornleigh Goes To It.*" On the Sundays I met Dick Lewis from Alton Manor Farm and we chatted over a midday meal, it was interesting for he had also joined the RAF and in fact was on his way to Birmingham when we parted company for good on the 22nd. We corresponded for while and then lost touch as happened with most of my short term pals, which was never the case with the close knit friendship of those back home, Cyril and Jonah in particular. My working hours during these last weeks, apart for the regular stint in the dairy, were largely spent in the arable fields planting cabbage seedlings, also singling the kale crop and others which had been drilled with seed; it was a time consuming manual work. I was just in time to experience treading the grain, the final three days in fact when truck loads of brewer's grains were delivered from the brewery at Burton on Trent. The grains, still fresh and warm were unloaded into a compound and three of us, wearing gum boots, spent all our time walking round and round compressing it to make room for the next delivery. A more boring job one could not imagine, I must have walked miles, the heat penetrated the boots making my feet hot and sweaty but at least the heady brewery smell was not unpleasant. It was a strange ending to my farming aspiration.

In these latter days at the farm my diary mentions yet another girl, Joan Wood who lived at 80 Victoria Avenue, Burrowash a village barely two miles north of Thulston, we must have met at the Harrington Arms when I was with my farming mates. She was very attractive and I made a date with her which happened to be the day I had the telegram from home, we met in the evening and having borrowed a bike we went for a cycle ride along the country lanes until 10.30. We met again the following evening knowing our short acquaintance had to end and we parted with promises to write but only one or two letters passed between us before the memory faded.

I had arranged with the Gaffer to leave the farm on the 26th June and the evening before my departure I took a suitcase to Derby railway station for deposit in the left-luggage, then returned in good time to have a farewell drink at the Harrington Arms with John, Ted, and of course Rose. I went back with her to No. 19 to say goodbye to her parents; it was a sad time on one hand and exciting anticipation on the other. Here again I promised to write but my second letter was to remain unanswered. It was the way of life, meeting and parting. In the morning I shook hands with the Gaffer and Mrs Hutchinson, thanked them for looking after me and hitched a lift to the railway station on the milk lorry. My departure from Thulston Fields did not have the same sentiment as leaving the Spencers at Alton Manor and my thoughts were soon set on the homeward journey. The guard blew his whistle and waved a green flag then the train puffed its way from the platform at just past nine, I was on my way home and used the railway warrant issued to me at Padgate. This was my third occasion of travelling on this line so I had become familiar with the London terminus, St Pancras, and found no problem getting on a bus with my luggage which took me to Victoria Station. I just had time to look at the indicator board and get to a train waiting on the platform before it set off and arrived in Brighton seventy seven minutes later at 2.45pm. It was surprising how well the country's transport still seemed to operate under the very difficult circumstances caused by air-raids and the blackout, but I doubt whether this was in my mind as I greeted my parents and immediately contacted Cyril and Jonah at their places of work so that I met them in the evening. I was very happy at being home again among family and friends; they were very much part of my life

A visit to the Ronuk office at Portslade on the following day went well, chatting to previous colleagues and staying to lunch in the hall, I doubted whether I would ever go back to working there although the future could not be foreseen. Naturally I went to church on Sunday morning, and then surprisingly had a swim at St Luke's Terrace school baths with Cyril and Jonah. We had the baths to ourselves and this was made possible because Jonah, who was like a fish in the water, knew the caretaker. The rest of the day was spent playing tennis and also golf at the Roedean course with other friends joining us. The next day Monday, 30th June I telephoned Stuckey & Carr the solicitors at 4 Pavilion Parade and contacted Joan Harrison, the girl who signed my autograph album which I briefly mentioned in November shortly before I had set off to the farm. There was apparently some reason for calling her "Bright Eyes" and we met later at 6.15 to visit the Odeon cinema in West Street. After the show I left her at the solicitor's office for she was apparently on fire watch duty that evening. It is almost as though these two meetings with this girl are a dream for, most unlike me, I made no note of her address or where she worked and neither did we ever correspond.

My farewell evening took place on the Wednesday when I met Cyril, Jonah and Frank at the Beaufort, we traversed the town calling in the Reeve Inn, Jimmy's (an Edlins Pub near the Old Steine), and the Greyhound in East Street, taking in a fish and chip shop en route. Cyril then suggested a visit to a girl friend on night duty at a First Aid Post (FAP) which was halfway up Bear Road. It was a long walk and we arrived about midnight, there was hardly any moon and the post was no more than a hut surrounded by sandbags but those on duty were pleased to see us. I recall this event well for we were all given a drink which had been spiked with bromide to sober us up. The girl in question was Gladys Searle who lived in Whitehawk Crescent and she had accompanied us three days earlier when we played tennis and golf. She was good company but I never got to know how she became associated with my group of friends and I only saw her on a few occasions when I was home on leave.

Two days later I was on my way to Blackpool having said goodbye to my parents who put on a brave face as they must have had worries at this time. Jonah accompanied me to the station and waved me off at 7.40; it was a fast train taking exactly one hour to reach Victoria. I then caught a bus to Euston Station, the L.M.S. terminus for the north-western counties, where I boarded the 10.25 to Preston and after a five hour journey I had only eight minutes to wait for the connection to Blackpool.

July 1941- June 1943

Life in the Royal Air Force Regiment

It was obvious that my train from Preston carried a good number of similar travellers and when it drew into Blackpool station at 4.30pm on Friday, 4th July we were met by RAF personnel who recorded our presence. Seventeen of us were counted out and we jumped in the back of a lorry which took us to a boarding house, No. 119 Church Street, an ideal location in the centre of the town. I was allocated to a room with three others and after getting settled in lost no time in going for a walk along the seafront. I was in Blackpool for six whole days; on day one all the arrivals assembled or rather paraded on the sea front and marched in an ungainly fashion to the Winter Gardens where we were kitted out with a uniform and other accoutrements, this was accomplished by walking along an endless row of tables and gradually accumulating the necessary individual items. We were also paid ten shillings (10/–) and had the rest of the weekend free to enjoy ourselves, it was a case of walking in the building as civilians and coming out as servicemen.

The week passed quickly with getting inoculated, vaccinated, identity tags and learning the elements of parade drill. In between times I really enjoyed the Pleasure Beach which was in full swing with the roller coaster, rides and stalls. The Tower complex with the Ballroom and Organ was also a compelling experience not to be missed. In fact, I was sorry to leave on Friday 11th when our group entitled "C" Squadron was inspected by an officer before marching to the station and taking a train to Morecambe. It was only a 75 minute ride and at 11.15 we were lining up at Morecambe station to be divided again into sections and, in a similar procedure to Blackpool, I landed up at 102 Clarendon Road in a room with four others. By design or otherwise one of my room mates, Jack Bradley, had been in the joining-up party which met at Derby, consequently his service number was just seven digits more than mine, we also had a lot in common so the time in Morecambe was enhanced by having a good pal.

All twelve of us at the billet were in No. 23 Flight which totalled 25 with a corporal in charge and we paraded on the promenade every day during the next four weeks or so, usually at 07.45 and again at 13.30. It was fascinating to watch the tide from the seafront which went out miles across the Bay until there was no sight of the water and then it came back again seemingly in a rush to cover the sand. The training programme was mostly marching drill with rifles (P14s) handed out to us when required, this activity on the promenade was interspaced with frequent visits to the Vickers Recreation Ground where we had bayonet practice, lectures and I fired ten rounds from the rifle on a 25 yard range. In the early days we were issued with PT kit which became well used with hours of physical training, including a long enjoyable run into the surrounding country with our very fit corporal. Every Sunday there was a Church Parade and I voluntarily went to the service which was held in a cinema, except one Sunday when I went to St John's Church on my own.

There was not a lot to do in the evening but walks about town interspaced with visits to the YMCA and the cinema with Jack provided breaks from staying in the billet. Several of those in the billet would congregate in one room nearly every night to play cards. The popular card game was "Bragg" gambling with copper coins; however I was wary of parting with money and only took part now and again to be friendly, but more often would keep occupied by writing letters. Cyril wrote to me on 27th from none other than 64 Coronation Street, Blackpool. He had told me a month back that he was going through the process of joining the RAF as a Wireless Operator/Air Gunner (WOp/AG). I never thought he would land up at Blackpool and miss me by only three weeks. It was a case of being 'so near yet so far' as it was not possible for me to leave Morecambe and I replied to that effect. His letter of four pages with the ink now faded was the first of 22 which were destined to remain forever in my memory.

Our billet in Clarendon Road left much to be desired with meals certainly not very edible, and these circumstances brought about a change of billet on the 1st August when we moved to 37 Victoria Street. The difference was remarkable, it was just like being at home and the food was first class, a pity we had not been taken here at the beginning for there was not much time left. I was paid one pound fifteen shillings (£1.15s) on the 7th and promptly

obtained a postal order for eight shillings and sent it to my
parents simply because I thought of them. It was about this
time that our Flight along with the others was being
individually tested and we demonstrated our new found
skills under the eagle eye of the Commanding Officer. Over
several days we satisfied the C.O. with our marching drill,
rifle drill, bayonet fighting and physical training. The latter
took place on the 9th when we were told that our Flight and
another, 50 of us in all, would be joining 812 Ground
Defence Squadron at Holme on Spalding Moor.
Arrangements were made to photograph each Flight and
also those in the separate billets; it was all very amicable as
we formed up in front of the camera. However, upon
receiving my copy of the prints I became aware of being the
only one with spectacles.

Ken with RAF No. 23 Flight, C. Squadron at Morecambe

Back at the billet there was much speculation about
the move for none of us knew where Holme on Spalding
Moor was, we waited for instructions and these were
forthcoming the next day at the Sunday church parade, we
would be moving out on Tuesday. It was a leisurely couple of
days for we had completed the course and the parades on
Monday were merely assemblies in preparation for the
morrow. I was paid one shilling and six pence (1/6d)
presumably this brought me up to date for the time at

Morecambe. In the afternoon we packed our kit and each received a pack of rations for sustenance during the journey. Parade next morning was at 5am so I had my head down early and those in our room did the same. The lady who looked after us at Victoria Street must have been up even earlier to prepare the breakfast and seemed sorry we were leaving; her concern over the welfare of her charges must have been above and beyond what recompense she received. I felt like giving her a hug as we all left the billet carrying new kit bags stamped with our service number.

The train left Morecambe station at 7am and there were several changes: Leeds, York and Market Weighton. Then there was a good hour's wait for the short six mile journey to the village railway station of Holme on Spalding Moor and our destination the RAF Station in Yorkshire which we reached at 15.00hrs. Our group when added to other arrivals totalled nearly 130 and No: 812 Defence Squadron was officially on the record as from August 12th, 1941. The RAF Station had also only just been completed and was building up to become operational.

Initially I was very disconcerted to find myself under the orders of army officers and NCOs who had been seconded to the RAF. I had never given it a thought that my RAF training with the Squadron would be in similar fashion to the infantry, but it was too late to change my mind. Our sleeping quarters at No. 2 Dispersal Site were a few wooden huts in a copse along the side of a narrow lane which led to the main buildings of the aerodrome a mile away. The other end of the lane joined the road between the village and the town of Goole; the distance to the former was only a few minutes walk whilst the latter was ten miles away. All the meals, parades, assemblies for duties took place at the main site, so there was much coming and going from the billets. Fortunately, drivers of vehicles passing along the lane often gave us lifts, not because we were lazy but to save time and keep ours boots clean, ready for inspection at the parades.

The first week commenced with getting used to our newly issued weapons, drill with P14 rifles and bayonets taking firing positions lying low, kneeling and standing. There were lectures on poison gas and hand grenades; also a trip round the assault course which I came to learn was standard army procedure, and was to encounter many different versions of this exercise. At the end of a run over the assault course it was usual to fix bayonets and attack several sacks filled with straw, some being suspended between posts and others lying on the ground; then quickly falling flat, fire a few blank rounds at an imaginary retreating enemy. In addition to the army training there were other duties or chores such as working in the cookhouse, the stores and even helping to sweep the main entrance.

The following week I was detailed in a working party and commenced digging trenches and sand-bagging ack-ack posts at strategic points around the airfield, preparing for any attack. We also went to a satellite station seven miles away at Breighton for several days to carry out similar defensive work. During the night of Sunday, 31st August, a stray German bomber showered the aerodrome with butterfly anti-personnel bombs. These devices were like bean cans and had rotating vanes at either end which sufficiently activated the detonator; so that some exploded on impact while others lay dormant until moved. Consequently there were some initial casualties and it was not until daybreak, when unsuspecting men started picking them up with fatal results, that the situation became apparent, a warning was then given out on the tannoy loudspeaker system. The Squadron was assembled to search the whole aerodrome and we combed the airfield in extended line and found quite a number; each one was carefully surrounded by sandbags and harmlessly detonated. This incident nearly coincided with the arrival of a squadron of Wimpeys (RAF slang for Wellington Bombers) and round the clock guard duties commenced.

I often found myself on the outskirts of the airfield at an ack-ack post, armed with a 1914-18 Lewis machine gun mounted on a stand. Between times the training continued; more goes over the assault course, lectures on the Lewis and Vickers machine guns and aircraft recognition. Two days were spent at Royston range near Hornsea, practice firing at various distances to 300 yards. We were now also guarding the bomb dump and the kites (RAF slang for aircraft) which were parked on their individual dispersal sites; there was one guard looking after two kites walking back and forth between them.

On the 17th September I started my first leave having previously filled in the necessary application, Form 295.

This coincided with a move to new quarters on the main site, Hut No. 107, a much better location for us and the change was completed before I left the station and hitch-hiked to York, even though I had a rail warrant for Brighton. It was my first experience of hitch-hiking and would certainly not be the last, for this was a good way of getting about without any expense and if there was no train or bus service, most drivers would stop if they had room in the vehicle. I caught the 18.02 from York which pulled into the London & North Eastern Railway terminus, Kings Cross Station at 00.15. The sun set during the journey and the carriages were lit by low wattage blue bulbs which made reading almost impossible, the blinds were also pulled down to black out the train. At each stop the name of the station was shouted out, above the speaker system if one was in operation, and it was necessary to remain alert for the required stop. Fortunately I was going to the end of the line so had no worry about missing a station. Somehow I made my way across London to Victoria and found the earliest train to Brighton was at 05.20; however I was directed to a nearby YMCA where I spent four hours in the company of many other servicemen.

Eventually I arrived home at 08.00 and proudly displayed my uniform to my parents. It was sheer luck that Dick Whittington was on leave at the same time so I had his unexpected company along with Jonah and other friends throughout. We visited all the old haunts and had many a drink in the Beaufort, Sunday 21st was a particular busy day I ran out of space in my diary; I served along with my father at the church service in the morning before meeting up with Jonah, Dick, Gladys and Frank. We went to watch an ice hockey match at the stadium then met up again after lunch to hear a military band which was playing in the Royal Pavilion Gardens, no doubt a morale booster for the town. The evening was spent at Sherry's Palais de Danse with Dick and Jonah, while there I bumped into Frances Commons an old flame from the past at a time when we had barely left school, as usual there was a promise to write but the correspondence never lasted beyond one letter.

Jonah and I accompanied Dick to the railway station on Tuesday 23rd and saw him on his way back to Harwell where he was under training as a WOp/AG the same as Cyril. The next day Jonah waved me away at 10.08 but I did not leave without a thought for my parents by noting in my diary *"I owe a lot to my darling Mum and Dad for a good leave."* My return journey went like clockwork and seemed faster, I suppose this is always the case when leaving those you love behind. However I was under orders and duly reported my presence to the guard room at the entrance to the RAF station well before the deadline of 23.59 hours, whereupon I found my bed space in Hut 107 and was soon in friendly banter with the other inmates.

The next day it was back to the training and guard duties, we were now learning the Morse code and field signals. On Sunday 28th I went to the village church in Holme for their Harvest Festival service and this did much to dispel my unrest at these recent days since returning from leave. Early in October an evening bus service to Goole left the station at 18.00 hours and returned at 23.00 hours. This made the small town accessible and it became a popular place to visit for there were some shops, a good YMCA and Toc H, three cinemas and a large market hall where a dance was held on Saturdays. I used the bus at the earliest opportunity and went to Goole on October 4th the first of a countless number of visits.

It was a change to spend two days constructing a small rifle range for the Home Guard at Londesborough, a small village north of Market Weighton. I was then fortunate to be detailed for three weeks' duty in the gas store, which entailed making up and issuing respirators and passing men through the gas chamber to test their effectiveness. The trick in this was to get them to remove their masks just before vacating the chamber so they came out coughing and crying from the effect of the gas, I knew all about the gas procedure from my experience when working at Ronuk and in the Home Guard. My session at the gas centre did not excuse me from guard duties and I was still on the roster for the Wimpeys, bomb dump and the AA guard with the old Lewis Gun. The station was now operational and the night Wimpey guard had to look after those kites not on missions. On nights when there was no moon to light the sky it was pitch black on the airfield and a very lonely job for the guards. When the engines of a kite had recently been working they would constantly make peculiar noises while the metal contracted or expanded as if trying to talk and ease the feeling of loneliness.

On the 21st October I eagerly opened a letter from home and was struck dumb by the unexpected information in the first few words that *"Dick was killed in a flying accident last Friday 17th."* I wrote in my diary *"This came as a great shock to me, the first one of the Boys to get killed – Horrible, very upset."* Fortunately the letter reached me at the end of the day so I had a while to let the news sink in and was immediately able to pen my thoughts back home and to Cyril. It was only just over four weeks since Frank had taken a photo of us together in Duke Street. We had spent a lot of time together, he was a good friend and my thoughts went back over the years to when he joined the JDL in 1938, supplying the oil lamp for the hut we used behind the church hall, playing Monopoly and Buccaneer. Strange that he never came camping with us but helped on one occasion by obtaining a very necessary ground sheet, small things like that bring to mind his good natured friendship.

Ken with friends in Duke Street a month before Dick's death

On the 24th October I heard from Cyril that he was going on leave, adding *"As it is now, I guess my leave is of secondary importance to me after hearing from Jonah ... I guess we are beginning to know what war is really like now.*

I know we all feel the same about Dick, and if possible will settle accounts for him." He hoped I could also get home but it was impossible. Three days later the Bomber Command Band turned up at the station and gave a performance; it was excellent and really good for the morale. Then I finished at the gas centre and submitted a 295 for the weekend which would give me 72 hours, long enough to get home. No doubt I would miss seeing Cyril but would at least get to Dick's memorial service.

The 295 took effect from Saturday and I left the Station at 09.00 hours, after coming off a bomb dump guard an hour previously. I hitch-hiked to York; this was easy for at Market Weighton there was a main road bringing vehicles from Hull, so I was able to get the 11.55 to Kings Cross. It was good to be able to catch up on some sleep during the journey which was now almost routine and with the usual change of stations I eventually arrived in Brighton. Jonah soon joined me and we met up with my parents at the Pier Hotel in Marine Parade. Sunday morning I was up early to go to church for the communion service with Jonah. We met later and joined up with Frank, Peggy and Stan to visit the ice stadium for the hockey match, it was a way of passing time for none of us felt like gaiety. Dick's Memorial Service was in the afternoon and there was as many there as could make it, a good gathering considering the war prevented attendance of some. Cyril for instance was upset, his leave had ended only a few days earlier so he just missed being at the service and seeing me. Owen had accompanied Dick's parents to Harwell Cemetery for the military funeral which he described as a very moving event. The object of my short visit had been fulfilled and the next day I made the reverse journey without trouble.

Although Holme was only 250 miles north of Brighton, the difference in the weather was considerable and at the station it was very rough, wet, windy and cold. On the first day back I was called to a fire in the gas clothing store and spent several hours salvaging the contents. The Regiment seemed to be used in this way whenever there was a need for labour as we finished the week moving tons of coke from trucks at Holme railway station to the aerodrome. I was shovelling all day but was back there a few hours later on an all night guard over three truck loads of bombs, which was more in keeping with our purpose; we used the waiting room for rest periods and kept the stove alight for warmth and brewing up. Somehow, poppies reached the aerodrome on 11th November; shades of the 1914/18 war, but the hour went by without notice. Although I had the day off owing to the night's guard it was not a happy one for me, for in the evening I breezed into the mess for something to eat, the place was nearly empty and much of it was in darkness. Someone had placed a seating form across the gangway, I tripped over it briefly knocking myself out and breaking the frame of my specs. I came to and staggered to the duty medical orderly who checked my bruised face and gave me some plaster to mend the specs; except for a black eye and a sore jaw I felt OK the next morning, nevertheless reported sick and the Medical Officer merely gave me a sight test for service spectacles.

There were frequent hut and kit inspections by either the C.O. or the Orderly Officer when everything had to be spick and span. The men in each hut were on a daily room orderly roster, so everyone took a turn at being responsible for the clean and tidy appearance of their hut. They also collected the mail, fuel for the stoves, cleaning material and other such jobs. At the kit inspections, everyone's equipment had to be laid out in similar fashion and in line with those on the next bed. Nothing was left to chance and a cord was stretched the length of the hut to ensure every item was in perfect line. There were incentives of extra time off for this chore, individually for having an extra neat kit layout, and collectively for having the cleanest hut. Hence I won a half day on the 14th November and hitch hiked into Goole with two mates for a visit to the cinema. On this occasion I saw the film "Boom Town" but my diary now often omits such detail.

The next day, being a Sunday I went to the church service which was held in the NAAFI and later watched a camp football match before getting ready for the Wimpey guard. At 01.30 hours I was called out of the rest room to Kite J which had caught fire, damaging the port engine and fuselage before it could be extinguished. This activity prevented us from resting and when the guard was stood down we were all excused further duty for the day. The end of the week I went into Goole with some of my hut mates and we wandered around the shops before having a snack in the YMCA and then going on to the Market Hall where the

Saturday night dance was taking place; we went in and mingled with the crowd. The atmosphere was great and the band churned out the music better than a jukebox, but I was apprehensive for dancing was not my forte, my knowledge was a few steps of the waltz.

The girls sat on chairs lined against the walls of the hall waiting for a man to ask them for a dance, and by chance I spotted an attractive girl who I recalled having seen a few hours earlier supervising the assistants behind the counters in Woolworth's. I plucked up courage, waited for a waltz and asked her for the dance. She was brilliant as I held her tight and shuffled around the floor taking all left hand turns and occasionally treading on her toes. We exchanged names and made small talk until after the dance and she was back in her chair, when I stood chatting a while getting to learn a little more about her. My thoughts were fixed on the announcement of the last waltz as I hung about waiting for another opportunity to ask her again, she accepted and there was laughter from her friends who had probably learned of my inaptitude at dancing. We came out of the Market Hall together and it was natural for me to ask if I could see her home, but she left me within seeing distance of the house after agreeing to meet again on Wednesday evening. The many special girlfriends who, in my teenage years, I thought I loved, were now just friends. This new acquaintance had captivated me from the moment I set eyes on her; little did I know at this time that Margaret would change the course and purpose of my life.

Back at the station I found the duty roster would prevent me from keeping the date, so I hastily wrote a note addressed to her at Woolworth's in Goole suggesting another time. She received the letter on Tuesday and replied immediately suggesting a meeting on Sunday outside Woolworth's at 19.00 hours, also I was given the phone number of the shop, Goole 171, which I could use in the evenings when she was on fire watch, so I took advantage of this to confirm our date.

Another aircraft caught fire just a week after the incident to J. This time it was early evening at 21.30 hours when Kite B caught alight and the fire was much more serious as the fuel tanks blew up and ammunition on board was exploding. Rumour was rife and I was glad not to have been on guard duty at that time. The fires had resulted from the peculiar method adopted to keep the kites engines warm in bitterly cold weather, a canvas tent was erected over each engine and an oil stove placed inside. The tents were similar to those used by telephone engineers when working on lines under the pavements, and the fierce wind had loosened the canvas which knocked over the stove setting the tent on fire. It was realised that the guards on the airfield had no means of communication with the guardroom and if an incident occurred there was an inevitable delay in raising the alarm. Consequently the night guard was doubled, one to each kite and in addition to our rifles we were issued with torches and whistles, and also a fire extinguisher was placed by the undercarriages. The double guard only lasted a week but we still retained the dubious equipment for communication which was never put to the test.

My charge during the week of the change was kite K – coincidentally my own initial but my thoughts were more about the ACH1 trade test I had taken during the day which would increase my status from the lowest level of Aircraft Hand 2nd class to 1st class and bring a pay increase. The whole Squadron had taken the test comprising oral and written questions along with the practical use of the rifle, the Lewis machine gun with the ring sight and aircraft recognition. Everyone was also interviewed by the C.O.

As arranged I met Margaret at Woolworth's on Sunday evening. I was so looking forward to seeing her again and was there well before seven. Fortunately the full moon was only three days away, its illumination with the absence of clouds always assisted the vision in the blacked out streets. I saw her walking towards me dead on time and held out my hand, touching hers and expressing pleasure at meeting her again. We joined arms and started walking and talking with her leading the way passed the Market Hall and cinemas to the river bank where the moon glistened on the water and the silent cranes at the docks were dimly visible skeletons. I lost count of time until at some stage we came off the river bank and started walking back along the road which ran alongside, then into the town to the one and only road of shops, Boothferry Road. The route here was the same as when I went partly home with her the previous week; a short way past the Market Hall and Woolworth's brought us to the Railway Station with a level crossing carrying the main line between Doncaster and Hull across the road. An underpass took us safely to the other side and we turned right into Pasture Road, it was a long road and a few minutes walk before we stopped just opposite where she lived, Number 171; we made a date for next Saturday before she went across the road, waving before going inside.

It was the beginning of December at the parade next morning when I learned of being reclassified ACH1 improving my weekly pay from 17s to £1.8s a difference of 11 shillings which made me rich. Fog blanketed the aerodrome and did not clear until the end of the week but the routine guards and training went on and on. Field exercises, bayonets, morse, village fighting, a room orderly duty, guards on the bomb dump and Wimpeys, a cross country run. At the end of the week I moved with B Flight to a different hut, No. 105, before going to Goole to see Margaret and this time we went to the Tower Cinema.

Startling news reached the Squadron on Monday 8th, the Japanese had launched an air raid on America's naval base at Pearl Harbour and this brought America into the war. I felt heartened because our country would now get help in our struggle against Germany for I considered America to be more associated with us than the foreigners across the Channel. Nevertheless I feared for my friend the Padre, who had written to Cyril last October advising that life in Kobe was becoming unsettled but he intended to remain there as long as possible. Two days later we heard that the Japanese had sunk two of our battleships off the coast of Malaya, H.M.S. Prince of Wales and H.M.S. Repulse; the war was now intensifying but all around me there was no despondency for everyone had faith in our cause and our leaders.

A night exercise towards the weekend on the outskirts of the airfield meant blackened faces as we learned how to move about in silence and communicate by signals and touches. This meant we had little sleep but needed to be alert in the morning to undergo live grenade practice, only one of us was allowed in the throwing trench with the instructor while the others kept behind a bunker. We knew the drill having been told about the procedure beforehand, even so it could be a little unnerving at first, especially when pulling the split pin out and knowing the whole thing would blow up in seconds after it was released from the hand. I did not think this was a good way to end a week of disastrous news except that it brought us to Saturday afternoon, and I hitch-hiked to Goole to see Margaret; again we went to the Tower cinema after she left work but first called at her home as she wanted give me a recent photo of herself. I could not have been happier to be given this token of our friendship for in my eyes she was breath taking and this portrait was destined to never leave my side wherever I went. Initially it was burning a hole in my jacket all the evening until I returned to the Drome and was able to study it better and fix it on the back of my locker door, which is always the pride of place for photos.

*That photograph
of Margaret.
December 1941*

I had written home and to Cyril, mentioning my new girlfriend and also to let them know I was commencing eight days leave on Tuesday, 16th December. Again Cyril could not get away so we would not meet up and when I left for Brighton, after seeing Margaret at work before catching the train from Goole station, I was not all that enthusiastic about the journey ahead. The leave followed much the same

pattern as before. My parents were obviously delighted to
see me and they thought a lot of Margaret's photo which I
had brought with me, we exchanged letters during the leave.
Jonah kept me company nearly every evening and it was
fortunate for me he was still too young to join Cyril and I in
the RAF. At the weekend we met up with Owen, Frank,
Peggy and the two sisters Phyl and Bet, the latter was on
leave from the WAAF and looked very smart in her uniform.
My feelings at travelling back to Goole on the 23rd were quite
joyful as upon arrival I walked to 171 and spent an hour
with Margaret before catching the transport back to the
Drome. The Enterprise and Silver Dawn Bus Company who
operated this special service for the RAF was very good but
stuck pretty well to their time-table and although I never
missed the evening bus there were some close calls.

Luck was with me, for after a day of bayonet practice
and drill with the Lewis and Vickers machine guns I was
able to get back to Goole the very next evening, Christmas
Eve. I was surprised when calling at 171; Margaret invited
me in, saying her parents would like to meet me. Taking off
my forage cap and gloves then wiping my shoes on the door
mat I followed her along the passage into a cosy warm back
room where her mum and dad were sitting comfortably by a
fire that had a surround with brass fire implements, horse
brasses either side and seasonal cards on the mantelpiece, a
scene which would have not been out of place on a
Christmas card. Obviously they were concerned about their
daughter's welfare and wanted to know who she had been
seeing so much of during the past month, but this thought
did not occur to me as I shook hands and entered into
conversation. Whatever I said must have gone down well as
from then on I had a second home, and as I left the house to
catch the bus we kissed for the first time.

The main event on Christmas day was dinner served
by the officers and Senior NCO's while we were seated in the
mess; it really was turkey with trimmings followed by
pudding, free cigarettes and cigars, enough to put us all in a
festive mood. I was on guard over Wimpeys C and G in the
evening for a couple of two hour sessions, but between times
I was able to look in at the concert and dance which was
taking place in the mess until the early hours.

The issue of khaki battle dress on the 30th December
heralded the Squadron's new look for 1942 although we still

retained the blue for special parades and walking out. In January the first snow fell, a warning of a hard winter. A social and debating society group was formed and met one evening a week in the gym, discussing such subjects as "reincarnation", "is money the root of all evil?", "dreams" and "after the war, what?" I went to as many of the meetings as possible as I enjoyed this type of gathering like our Youth Club at home. We had a walking race between the Flights one Saturday morning and ours had the most men up front, including myself in sixth place. At every opportunity I went into Goole to see Margaret and when I returned on the evening of the 19th it was snowing hard so there was no surprise to find it laying very deep in the morning. Movement around the aerodrome was very difficult until the clearing operation got underway, all of us in the Squadron were issued with shovels and we started on the runway. A few heavy vehicles had a curved steel plate attached to the front which scraped the snow into heaps, and our job was to load it into trucks. There was a hell of a lot of snow on the airfield and more up in the sky, we were shovelling for three days. Then on Friday 23rd it poured with rain and turned the station into a lake so our labour was transferred to clearing the drains.

There was no training activity during that week; nevertheless I started the trade test for the next step up which was reclassification to Leading Aircraftman (LAC), and I joined the others who had become AC1s. As with the previous test it was part practical, written and oral with another interview with the C.O. There was a revision of the rifle and Lewis MG with the addition of the Vickers MG, grenades, military tactics and fire orders. By this time I knew the weapons text book by heart, their weight, range, rate of fire, drill for clearance of stoppages, and could strip and assemble them blindfolded. At the interview the C.O. asked me if I had ever thought becoming an officer and seemed disappointed when he discovered I was too young at nineteen, but I was not that ambitious. Again like at the time of the AC1 test, I was on guard duty during the night; it was the first one operating another procedure, the guard were now equipped with cycles and had to patrol the airfield in pairs, the weather was lousy for cycling. After coming off the guard the next morning I took an aircraft recognition test which was the final LAC session, and the result was quick in coming through. I learned of the pass on the 27th but the classification did not become effective until February 1st when I must admit I was rather pleased with the job I made of sewing the propeller badge on my uniform.

It was also on the 1st February 1942 that the Royal Air Force Regiment came into being by Royal Warrant of His Majesty King George VI when it was constituted as a corps within the Royal Air Force in order to defend the airfields. We were issued with "RAF Regiment" shoulder insignia to sew on our uniforms and the Squadron was renamed 2812 Squadron RAF Regiment, the army personnel transferred to the RAF so the C.O. Lt Fred Gould became a Squadron Leader. It seemed a natural transition. The extra three shillings a week which came with my propeller badge would come in handy, and perhaps more important I was beginning to become accustomed to the way of life, the discipline and comradeship which surrounded me at the station. This state of mind was also probably due to the close presence of Margaret whom I saw frequently. Additionally I had a dozen addresses for correspondence headed by Cyril, and a number were girls who I suppose wrote more or less to keep the spirits up.

Snow persisted on and off in February so the Squadron spent much time shovelling. On the 3rd we were called out at 21.00hrs and worked until 01.30hrs clearing the runway by the light of a nearly full moon. This effort earned us a rum ration in a similar way to the navy splicing the mainbrace but we also had a hot meal in the mess. The kites based at the station were not currently being flown on operational missions and this snow clearance appeared to be for emergency use. All the LACs were now called upon to do an orderly corporal duty and when it was my turn I had to see the men were roused in the morning and attend the morning and afternoon parades, the guard parade at 17.00hrs, staff parade at 22.00hrs, and ensure the lights were out at 22.30hrs. In between times it was a matter of being at the Orderly Officer's beck and call.

There were three route marches during the month each about twenty miles and one of them was to Goole and back. When we reached the outskirts of Goole, the C.O. joined the squadron from a motor vehicle, he had us shoulder arms and with him at the head we marched through the town to the clock tower. We were dismissed for an hour before re-assembling and returning in similar fashion. A lot of people stopped to watch us as we went through the town's main road but Margaret could not leave the shop. We also started training with a new piece of armament, the Smith Gun. This resembled a drain pipe between two large dustbin lids because the wheels were conical, and when tipped on its side one wheel formed the base and the other became the canopy. The barrel was smooth like a mortar and the contraption was cumbersome to handle, it could well have been a weapon invented for the Home Guard.

The last snow of the winter was cleared away early in March and the evenings were becoming lighter, our specific sentry duty on the Wimpeys was withdrawn leaving only the airfield cycle patrol. On Friday 13th I was detailed in a working party to get things ready for a visit by some top brass on Sunday and we were cleaning up and rehearsing up to the last minute. Sunday, the big day, commenced with a church parade and it took forty minutes of red-tape procedure before we could get inside the church for the service. When this had finished I joined a group detailed for a practice run over the assault course, while the top brass toured the airfield. After lunch we put on our assault course display for the benefit of Air Commodore Higgins, a Brigadier and other Officers. I thought it a good show and that we were all as mad as March Hares, if I had not been going on nine days leave on the following Wednesday I would probably have not been so cheerful.

This leave was special for even though I would miss my girlfriend I was hoping to meet up with Cyril who was now stationed RAF Tangmere only 30 miles from Brighton. Before leaving I saw Margaret at the shop then caught a train and eventually arrived home very late in the evening but expectant for the next day. Indeed the anticipation came to pass when along with Jonah we met Cyril at the station when his train pulled in at 17.00hrs; the three of us were together again after a break of nine months. We first went to see his parents and then painted the town red by visiting many of our old haunts before getting back to my house, and here we stayed all night beside the fire talking of past memories until seeing Cyril off on a train back to Tangmere at six in the morning. The meeting diminished the remainder of the leave and I was pleased to get back Goole and see Margaret before returning to the aerodrome.

April opened with a route march and a viewing of captured German air force equipment. All the usual activities went on and on. We marched to Market Weighton and marched back again several times but this was now easy. A course of first aid lectures proved very interesting and a helpful revival of my Boy Scouts badge. I went again to Rolston Range near Hornsea, firing the rifle and Lewis M/G and this time I took a turn in the butts signalling the hits on the targets. The C.O. provided an incentive by giving a half day off to the occupants of the cleanest hut and we gained one on Friday, 1st May. This enabled me to leave the Drome early on a long weekend pass for I knew Cyril was still at Tangmere. In order to save money as railway warrants were not issued with passes I decided to hitch-hike to London. It was quite a performance. I managed to reach Bawtry at 18.30 which put me on the A1 route to London and was fortunate in making my way down this busy road, with very few hitches, all the way to Edgeware Road, London where I was set down at 02.00. An all-night bus took me to Charing Cross where I slept in the underground for a few hours. Big Ben's hands were at 06.00 as I walked passed Parliament Buildings to Victoria and the 6.41 train got me home at 09.15. After a bath I was no worse for the journey in fact I had rather enjoyed myself.

The purpose of my visit was fulfilled the next day, Sunday 3rd when together with Jonah we took a train to Chichester and met Cyril who had come in from Tangmere about four miles away. We walked around the town, had some tea and Cyril took us to the pub they frequent. We reluctantly parted company to catch the 21.45 back to Brighton and en route my stomach, containing a mixture of beer with port wine decided to revolt. Jonah patted my back as I leaned over the loo in the train and then somehow got me safely back indoors at 12A. I had learned a lesson. Cyril's next letter refers to the incident *"I was awfully pleased and grateful to feel you gave up such a lot of valuable time to come over to see me. I hope the after effects were not too bad, I mean, to come nearly two hundred miles just to get a hangover isn't my idea of a joke."* He had been home and seen Jonah who had related the event.

Everything round about the aerodrome was very quiet with the station being non operational, nothing appeared to be happening and it was difficult to see that we were doing much to help the war effort. Having to Blanco our gas mask cases did very little for our morale. Towards the end of May, I reached the ripe old age of 20. All the lads in the hut had signed a card which read "*With love from the Boys of Hut 105 to our dearest virgin (Ken)*" The twenty-two signatories exaggerated their ranks and military decorations after their names, and I knew I was being ragged but took it in good heart and was, if anything, rather flattered they bothered about me. I was a regular visitor to Goole so it was no surprise that I saw my girl friend, Margaret, on my birthday day and had a special tea laid on for me by her mother. The weather was stormy so it was pleasing to stay in and play cards with her parents until it was time to catch the bus.

On Monday, 1st June I was detailed for duty in one of the hangers lending a hand to unload bicycles which were being transferred from railway trucks at Holme station. There were 480 of them so it was no mean job, especially separating them from each other as the handle bars and pedals became interlocked when loaded at the other end. The job occupied our working party most of the day and I have no recollection of seeing the bikes again or who used them as we already had bikes for our guard duties. A sign that better armament was on its way was given when we started constructing sites for the Hispano gun which fired 20mm cannon shells. The improved weather conditions made guard duties less arduous and it could be quite pleasant on the outskirts of the airfield. I particularly observed that bees, butterflies and skylarks had made their appearance during April, and in May I heard the cuckoo and discovered some partridge eggs. June was turning out to be warm and on the first Saturday afternoon hitch-hiking to Goole proved hopeless, the road was crowded with men from the Drome intent on doing the same thing. The ten miles took me two and a half hours so I must have walked all the way.

I had now been at Holme for nine months. The training and duties had become routine, I accepted that the once arduous assault course or twenty mile route march was no sweat. The fine weather, the absence of enemy planes, and my girlfriend close by – to say I was lucky was an under statement. Even so I always knew this idyllic state of affairs would not last. On the 15th June I was on my way to RAF Station Hemswell for a 14 day leadership course, with little knowledge as to what it was all about. The journey to Hemswell took a long time as for some inexplicable reason I travelled from Holme railway station at 07.30 to Leeds, thence by Retford to Gainsborough and by bus to Hemswell checking in at No. 1 Group Airfield Defence School at 17.00hrs. It would have been a quicker journey to have started at Goole.

Hemswell RAF Station is situated ten miles north of Lincoln straight along the Roman road (Ermine Street). A purpose built pre-war establishment with four larg hangers which separated the actual airfield from the numerous support buildings. Brick built two storey barrack blocks and the Headquarters surrounded the Parade Ground, it was all most impressive in comparison to Holme. However the school's quarters were in the usual wooden huts which had been erected on the fringe of the main site. There were billets for the course students, small classrooms for sectional instruction, a Nissen hut for general assembly and a small office building. There were about 24 of us on the course which was specifically designed for leadership training and run by army personnel, an officer and N.C.O. instructors. There was also the occasional appearance of Lt. Col. Murray who seemed to be in overall charge of the Defence Units in No. 1 Group Bomber Command. He was a stocky Scot who always wore a kilt and was forever munching seeds of grain which he kept in his sporran. On one instance during the course, the Colonel was with us when we had to climb up the vertical iron ladder which was fixed to the wall of the water tower. Naturally we stepped back for him to proceed first but he gruffly waved us on ahead because, as he put it, there was nothing under his kilt. When reaching to top of the tower, we all had an excellent view – of the airfield, of course.

At the commencement of the course we were split into three sections of eight men, each section had an instructor. The programme was a variation on the theme of my training at Holme. Sometimes each section did their own thing and at other times we operated as a group. There were numerous drill sessions on the station's Parade Ground and we took turns in shouting out the marching orders. We were loaded down with text books for lectures on map reading, field craft, infantry training, grenades and small arms. A sand table was used for discussions on battle tactics. Most of the practical exercises took place at Harpswell, a small village close to the airfield, where both an assault course and blitz course had been constructed on land nearby. The assault course was similar to that at Holme but the Blitz course was a new stunt to me. It was over a mile of planned attack exercises involving all of us on the course. The school had three AC2 assistants who acted as enemy and were positioned at places along the route, so whenever they fired (blanks) at us we had to locate their position and plan an attack. During the exercise, apart from hedges, ditches, and cow dung, there was a particular greasy tree trunk across a muddy stream where an officer enjoyed himself sticking thunder-flashes in the mud as we negotiated the crossing. Other obstacles included were an eight foot wall which required team work to traverse and a waist high stretch of water to wade through. Not everyone made it to the finish but we all returned to the huts wet through and up to our ears in mud. Then everything had to be washed and clean ready for parade next morning.

Ten days into the course, Thursday, 25th June 1942, we were given an examination on a variety of tactical situations, orders and map reading. The next day, after a free afternoon we waited until midnight before setting off on a route march to a place called Roman Hole which was seventeen miles away. We arrived there at 05.30hrs and immediately went into an attack exercise using live ammunition, an operation lasting four hours. Fortunately the return journey was made easy by having transport available to take us back to the aerodrome. Roman Hole was ideal terrain for the exercise, a deep long valley with patches of gorse or shrub scattered about its length and a few desolate farm buildings at one end. Exercise "Home Guard" was far better than my earlier experience at Brighton. We were all supplied with bicycles and had to pedal power to various map references in order to engage with paratroopers who had been dropped to destroy some important bridge or building. Finally, the two weeks were brought to an end with another session round the Blitz course and a general discussion in the Nissen hut. Having packed my kit the previous evening, I left Hemswell on Tuesday, 30th June catching a bus to Gainsborough and thence by train to reach Holme at 15.30hrs. I reported my presence and was able to get to Goole; it was the first thing on my mind, to see my girlfriend, nineteen letters had passed between us during the two weeks at Hemswell.

Two days later I was unexpectedly given seven days leave, however I was in no hurry to get to Brighton, preferring instead to linger in Goole with Margaret. Eventually I had to start making my way home and caught the 21.00hrs train to Doncaster. It was never a happy moment waving to her from the open carriage window of the train as it puffed out of the station amid a cloud of steam, but when she was out of sight I pulled up the window with the leather strap and sat down in resignation of another long haul. Upon reaching Doncaster, I whiled away the time at the YMCA which was nearby and then caught the 23.21hrs train to Kings Cross. I must have had a comfortable seat on the train and have been very tired for I slept throughout the four and a half hour journey to London; the train was blacked out with the blinds drawn and the pale blue lighting which made conditions ideal for sleeping. The coaches on the mainline had a corridor along one side with the doors at each end and the passenger compartments in between, so I remained undisturbed by the four intermediary stops and there was no worry about passing my destination as Kings Cross was the terminus. Someone shook my shoulder when the engine came to a standstill at the platform.

As I walked towards the ticket barrier I passed the massive engine which had hauled the twelve coaches from the North. It was still spitting steam and there was a canvas canopy from the roof of the footplate area to the coal tender, under which the driver and fireman was just visible. I should have given them more thought for their hard work but I was now accustomed to this sort of journey and took it all for granted. Again I was in the City during the early morning as it was only just past 04.00 hours and not yet light; without any thought of buses or the underground I strolled through the streets gradually making my way to Victoria more leisurely than on previous occasions. There were destroyed and damaged buildings at every turn and in many places where there had been a building or a suitable space, a brick built water reservoir had been constructed for emergency use. Thousands of sandbags were in evidence as protection against the blast of bombs and shrapnel, particularly in Whitehall where all the buildings were surrounded by sandbags up to the first floor. I adjusted my watch with the time of Big Ben at 05.30hours and in the dawn of the day I turned along Victoria Street towards the station to catch the 06.41 hours to Brighton.

Cyril was still at Tangmere and this time was able to come home at the weekends so the three of us were together again along with other friends. While out walking, by chance we passed Jerome's photographers in Western Road and Cyril suggested having our meeting recorded so in we went and were set up before the camera to produce a rare photo.

The JDL (Jonah, Cyril and Ken) together with Frank and Peggy - July 1942

It was a coincidence we both returned to our units on the same day, Saturday, 11th July; this was made possible because I applied for a 48 hour extension to dig my father's allotment. Jonah came to the station and we waved Cyril off at 10.17, then I left at 11.08. After being back at the Drome for two days I was called before the C.O. who conveyed the pleasing report he had received of my effort during the course at Hemswell. I was also given a hint that I would be staying at Holme when the Squadron moved out. A few days later I was interviewed by Lt. Col. Murray who confirmed I would be remaining at Holme, he also raised the question of a commission and fortunately I was still too young. At a special parade in the afternoon the Colonel delivered a speech and told everyone that the Squadron would shortly be moving to a much better aerodrome. The prospect of a change after eleven months at Holme was good news to most of the men and there was much speculation. Nevertheless I was content to stay and be near to Goole where my heart was.

For a good week after the Colonel's visit it seemed I was left to my own devices, except for two five hours stints in the cookhouse. Why I had this duty or what I did evades my memory and is not recorded. Maybe the pending move had upset the pattern of things or it might have been due to the fact I was not going with the main force. The job could have been spud bashing, cleaning the gear or stoking the coal fired ovens, one thing is for certain, I would not have done any cooking. It did not bother me especially as it gave me a lot of spare time to see Margaret. The last three days of the month I spent at the Breighton satellite airfield only a few miles away, slightly north of Howden. A small detachment of our Squadron was stationed there including Jack Bradley my mate at Morecambe. During my time at Breighton I was only on guard for one period of 24 hours, standing by with twin Lewis machine guns. There was an enemy aircraft alert but no sign or sound of anything unusual; daylight warnings had become common over the past few weeks due to the German hit and run tactics. Upon my return to Holme on Friday 31st I found the squadron had received its marching orders. The majority of the men were busy loading their kit on lorries and amid shouts and cheers 2812 Squadron embussed and moved out to RAF Coltishall, leaving behind six corporals and thirty men including yours truly with an officer and a sergeant in charge.

A letter from Cyril was also awaiting me from No. 1 Aircrew Wing, RAF Madley, Hereford where he had moved for more training. In relating the experience of his first flight he wrote *"The weather was lovely, good blue sky with billowy clouds. We were done up in flying jackets and harness, bags of zip fasteners everywhere. Then we climbed in and sat down in comfortable but compact seats. The engines were by now revving up and we moved forward around the perimeter to the runway. The engines roared and we increased speed and the next thing I knew was that we were above the 'drome. I looked down to a new world of dots and squares; we climbed gradually and eventually reached the cloud level, I felt alright and after swallowing once or twice the buzzing left my ears. I felt in a very "devil may care" mood something most of the chaps do... thinking it over I enjoyed it immensely."*

I immediately felt lonely when the Squadron left for I missed some very good comrades, yet on the other hand I was pleased to remain and be near Margaret. However the mood soon passed and I became more settled into a routine of A.A. guard duties which were more frequent because there were fewer names on the roster. It was a matter of 24 hours on and 24 hours off with odd jobs during the off period. The banks were closed on Monday, 3rd August when a lone German hit and run raider tried to open them in Goole at 10.00hrs by dropping some bombs about the town. This was a most unusual incident and there were many worried faces when I arrived in the afternoon, but I went to the cinema with Margaret and we watched the film *"Appointment for Love"* which made the bombing incident recede in the mind. This could have been the same lone raider which appeared twice in the vicinity of our aerodrome on the 8th and 9th. No attack was made, nevertheless on the first day I was on guard with the Hispano Cannon and I took the liberty of firing a few 20mm rounds towards his vanishing tail, with no chance whatever of doing any damage. It was an excuse to have a go but I was not to get another opportunity. On the 26th August 1942 I was attached without any warning to No. 1 Group Airfield Defence School, Hemswell, as an instructor. I just managed to ring Margaret and convey the news before motor transport took me to Selby railway station. The move took me by surprise for I had not been told beforehand but I had no trepidations as the two week course had made me familiar with what lay ahead. My one regret was leaving Goole but I would not be far away and the mail could be relied upon so we naturally commenced writing to each other between my leaves and passes. Little did we realise this would eventually result in a total of 1260 written communications passing between us.

Initially three of us arrived at Hemswell to take over the Defence School; the other two were Pilot Officer (P/O) Alan Appleby and Corporal Ron Harrison who came along with me from Holme. Other NCOs joined us but for shorter periods keeping our number to four. We also had four men on general duties assisting the field work when necessary. The Army supervised our take-over and left us a month later on 26th September after we had fully completed a course on our own. We continued in the same format, but as luck would have it the school had a break at the end of the very next session and I was given eight days' leave which I knew would again partly coincide with Cyril who was now Sergeant Wop/AG, still training at RAF Atherstone, Stratford. Jonah had also joined the RAF so he would be absent this time and so would Owen who had now become a boffin and was working at an explosives establishment in Scotland.

It was a strange feeling travelling South via Lincoln and Grantham without first seeing Margaret so when I arrived home on Friday, 9th October I wrote to her the next day, adding bits on Sunday and Monday before posting it so I was able to tell her about meeting up with Cyril over the weekend. Shortly after I had posted the letter a number of fighter bombers raided Brighton; one of the bombs went off near my grandmother's home No. 8 Rose Hill Terrace and blew her windows out. Cyril and I went to see if she was OK and found her sweeping up the glass. She was too elderly to understand what had happened and just remarked that somebody had broken her windows. It was also my parents' 35th wedding anniversary. Early in the evening I met Cyril's girlfriend, Raie for the first time and we had some great moments visiting the Eight Bells, Gizzi's, and lastly Jimmy's Blue Room in the company of his mother, my Aunt Lottie, and my brother and sister in law. This was a great finale before seeing Cyril off to Stratford from the station on the 13.08 the next day. Raie was also there; I shook her hand and expressed good wishes before turning down Trafalgar Street towards St Peter's Church, not knowing what the future had in store for us.

I left Brighton on the 16th, the same day that our friend and mentor, the Padre Oscar Brooks arrived in England having been repatriated from Japan. Although he had suffered a harrowing time news of his arrival certainly cheered me up during an uneventful journey to Hemswell. The courses continued straight away, receiving another batch of students who came from various aerodromes in No. 7 Group. We took no part in their attachment, we only had a list of names and units so we would know who to expect. While they were in our hands we had complete control over their lives throughout the length of the course. At times I felt at a disadvantage as my LAC badge did not portray much in the way of superiority for giving orders, it was not a badge of rank, but I had been given a hint this was to be addressed. In my spare time I was busy making a ring out of a piece of perspex taken from a damaged aircraft's gun turret. This thick clear material could easily be filed, engraved and polished and just required patience. I pierced a hole in the centre of a small piece with a red hot poker, then after much filing, smoothing with emery paper and polishing with Brasso somehow managed to carve the initials JDK on it to indicate Jonah, Douglas (Cyril's first Christian name), and myself, Ken. I sent it to Cyril and he replied *"...it's funny but I kind of thought the world of it from the minute I first saw it. I'll always wear it Ken, it's more than just a ring it's everything you have and still mean to me."*

Ken's Portrait – October 1942

On the 26th October I learned of my promotion to Corporal which was back dated to the 9th. It was pleasing news so I enjoyed replacing the LAC badge on my uniform with the twin tapes and went to the camp photographer and had a photo taken for Margaret.

I found a cheap way to get to Goole without using the train whenever I had the time between courses by walking to the main Lincoln Road and hitch hiking in the other direction. This led north to Scunthorpe and from there along a minor road through Crowle and Swinefleet to the level crossing at Goole Station, the one snag was the lack of vehicles on the minor road which delayed the journey but it was a good route. Not once was Margaret out of my thoughts and I was concerned when she told me she was joining the Women's Land Army. She was going for training in Somerset on the 14th December and knowing how tough farming could be I did wonder how she would cope along with leaving home for the first time, especially with Christmas in the offing.

At Hemswell, a course conveniently ended on the 19th; we shut up shop for Christmas and I went on leave. Seven days in Brighton and not one of my friends was in town, I even missed seeing Frank who could not join the forces, so perhaps he was having a holiday; my time was therefore occupied with the family, to be able to go to St Luke's with them throughout the festival was a bonus. My parents came to the station with me, their first time to see me away on Boxing Day, a Saturday.

I had plenty to start my new 1943 diary for instead of continuing with the courses the three of us met up in the Defence Office for instructions. Alan Appleby had been promoted to a Flight Lieutenant (F/Lt) and Ron Harrison to a Sergeant (Sgt) and they were destined to go for three weeks to the Army's 48th Division Battle School on the 5th January. This particular course was for officers and senior NCOs and Alan was concerned about leaving me kicking my heels at Hemswell while they were away, so he had the brilliant idea of taking me with them as his batman. We duly travelled to Brocklesby Park, Habrough, Lincs the home of the Earl of Yarborough, where the Divisional Battle School was well installed. Upon arrival at the Guard Room I caused some head-scratching for they were in quandary on how to billet a Corporal Batman. I waited about until Alan came rushing back saying it was all OK he had got me on the course, this news relieved the check-in clerk who promptly directed me to a hut along with the sergeants.

I was unprepared and did not have much spare kit for this venture but there was nothing I could do to change things. The experience of the next three weeks made our Defence School at Hemswell seem like a holiday camp. To make matters worse it was mid-winter, very cold and rained most days, I had little in the way of spare kit and often had to start the day in damp clothing. We had exercises night and day using live ammunition, river crossing by night in pouring rain, wood clearing, village fighting, rock climbing, etc. On the final day we were dumped individually around the country, with nothing but a map and instructions to rendezvous at a reference point ten miles away without getting picked up; this was deliberately sited beyond a main road which needed to be crossed and was well patrolled, therefore the unwary were caught. Even with all this I managed to get to Goole when we were given a weekend break during the course. Margaret had returned home after a harrowing posting to Wales following the training at Somerset, so I was able to be with her for a few hours.

We returned from Brocklesby Park at the start of February and spent two days with our C.O. Lt Colonel Murray who drove us around the locality, surveying the ground and meeting up with farmers for the purpose of planning a two-week course on the lines of our experience at Brocklesby Park. The school's title was also changed to No. 1 Group Battle School, using a new programme commencing 4th February. I had been very surprised to receive a lettercard from Cyril while I was at Brocklesby, he had addressed it to RAF Regiment Students Course, 48th Divisional Battle School, Home Forces, and although he got the course wrong it found me. He was in Brighton for 14 days and like me found there were no bosom pals around but Raie, to whom he was now engaged, and who was due to spend the last nine days with him so he had something to look forward to. He was returning to Yorkshire and suggested a possible meeting but he went to Leeming and then Middleton St George which was far from my posting so we were unable to meet.

Our new Battle School Courses started well and the C.O. came over from the Group H.Q. at Bawtry several times to observe progress. He had procured a collapsible boat from the Army for our night river crossing scheme, we used a large pond and the noise must have caused disturbance to nearby inhabitants but they were all informed of our operation. One of the regular all day schemes was an attack exercise in the area of Walesby and Tealsby, small villages 14 miles east of the drome, around here there was a lovely stream, rippling through the fields with fresh water good enough to drink. Our exercise covered this water course and the men had to walk along it for some distance; whenever I was there the terrain always made me think of Tennyson's poem *The Brook*. We only managed to complete two courses before our quarterly leave became due and this time I had persuaded Margaret's parents to let her come home with me so we set off for Brighton on Sunday, 7th March.

I walked her across London to see the sights, the Parliament Building and Big Ben in particular as we had time to spare before catching the train and arriving home at 19.30hrs. The weather was very kind and we were able to cover a lot of ground walking the Downs to Newmarket Copse where we picked violets, also going to Ovingdean, the seafront and parks. We met up with the Padre, I had already told Margaret all about him and it was good to learn he was to be inducted as the Vicar of Rye Church in a few weeks on the 30th. As for entertainment, we visited the Savoy, Regent and Academy cinemas, finishing the last evening at the Imperial Theatre in North Street to see the play *"Rain"*. This was my first visit to the Imperial which was under construction at the start of the war and opened in April 1940. I did not take much notice of the interior except to think it was spacious and modern.

The return journey was started earlier in the morning and got us back in Goole at 15.00hrs on Saturday 13th, I was made welcome but Margaret was very tired and I was unhappy having to report back to Hemswell the following day. This visit to Brighton by Margaret would turn out to be a blessing.

Ron and I saw the C.O. upon our return and were informed that our officer was sick, the next course would therefore go ahead without him, so, along with another Corporal, the three of us did just that, which took us into

April. Cyril was now at Middleton St George flying with Canadians in 419 Squadron and we were writing often, exchanging more of our innermost thoughts than would be conveyed to anyone else. I feared for him on his dangerous missions and did my utmost to instil hope and encouragement in my words, at least his replies always led me to believe I succeeded when I read "*As usual it was a wizard letter I had from you – I always feel after reading one of your letters – well I guess things aren't so bad when there are people like that around.*" I heard from him at the end of March and early April, he told me about losing the JDK ring which needed to be sawn off as he had sprained his hand, alas I did not get time to make another. Perhaps more importantly he asked me to be best man at his wedding to Raie on May 1st, this meant more to me than words could express but I knew this date would coincide with a course and I had to apologise.

The frequency of our school's visits to the Walesby area resulted in us becoming friendly with the villagers and, with their help, our officer came up with the idea of a scheme which involved staying there a couple of nights using the Village Institute which was their community hall. Better still, we were to hold a dance in the hall on the second night with the villagers arranging the advertising and music while we were to provide the refreshments. The plan was first put into operation on the course commencing Good Friday, 23rd April. We marched the men to Walesby on the following Friday, a distance of twelve miles, carried out the field exercises and on the Saturday evening held the dance which was a roaring success, especially with the Land Army girls. I was in charge of the finance and sold some of our rations, cheese sandwiches for one shilling with all the profits going towards the upkeep of the Institute. I must have got along with the folk very well as there was an occasion one evening when one of them lent me his 410 shotgun; I returned from walking round the fields with two rabbits and a rook. Margaret also addressed her mail to me c/o The Post Office, Walesby, such were the wonders of the Royal Mail when letters sent from Goole postmarked 7.45pm reached me the next day at 8.00am.

We were at Walesby on Cyril's wedding day, May 1st. They would have received the greetings telegram I sent to 29 Boundary Road, Hove 3, and I had a drink, during the dance in the evening to give them a thought, as he had suggested. The wedding took place at the Register Office and even my absence at the event did not prevent our affiliation being recorded, for the local newspaper's account of the ceremony reported me as supporting the couple. It was almost as though a spiritual force linked us together, which was shortly to become even more apparent.

Cyril in his flying kit –
October 1942

The musings in our letters took us back to the early 1930s, the start of the JDL, the camps at Church Farm, the midnight hikes, boating on the river from the Anchor Hotel, Spithurst, Isfield, and the home church of St Luke. Our youthful days were relived in our correspondence, but in between it took a different turn when he described his flying activity:-

> "I've done another two - Duisburg and St. Nazaire
> last night and it was pretty well touch and go –
> running the gauntlet over the target is pretty grim,

*it is just touch and go whether you will make it or
not. It was a hell of a mess when we got there,
and as we made our run up the flack lessened
then directly we got over, the b******* let us have
it, these two minutes seemed like an eternity. We
beat them all and dropped our bombs in the
middle of an area of seething fires that looked like
molten metal bubbling and spluttering. Already
we have had the luck of the devil. At Duisburg we
were flying in the area for 40 minutes, 35 minutes
longer than the proper time, but the Bomb Aimer is
a keen type and seems to have a personal grudge
against the Jerries. I've lost lots of my pals and
although there is no immediate effect I guess I will
get it later on."*

There is little wonder I feared for him and was
unsettled knowing that my role at Hemswell although
strenuous did not put me in any danger, it seemed unfair.
Early in May I managed a couple of days off between courses
to see Margaret who was billeted in Leeds for a few weeks
while on an engineering course training to work in an
aircraft factory at Brough near Goole. My 21st birthday on
the 26th did not go unnoticed by the dozen cards I received
in the post but otherwise was a routine day. At Hemswell
our programmes incorporating the Walesby dances were
held on two more occasions, the last being the 4th June
before the course ended five days later. Then we were given
eight days' leave with no knowledge as to whether the school
would continue upon our return. I was reluctant to go home
for my heart was now with Margaret in Goole. I travelled to
see her, stayed overnight and did not leave until late Friday
evening 11th June, writing in my diary *"I did not feel like
parting with all that I love so dear but I have a home and
parents to whom I owe so much and love in a different way."*
I journeyed through the night arriving home early Saturday
morning to a quiet day, an evening out with my parents at
the Odeon, then writing an unfinished letter to Margaret
before I had to get some sleep.

I awoke to Whit Sunday, 13th June 1943 to a pleasant
day as I walked to St Luke's for the 8am communion service.
Uncle Stan and Aunt Lottie were there and after the service
they informed me that Cyril had been reported missing from

an operation on Friday night when 43 of our planes failed to return. I went with them across the road by the Pepperbox where there was a telephone kiosk and helped to ring Raie for she did not yet know; her marriage was so recent the records had not been updated to show her as the next of kin. Upon arriving home I went to my room and through my tears added words to my letter telling Margaret how unhappy I was. I wished I could have been with him on his flights. I met Jonah and Frank at midday and we were a very subdued trio lunching in Edlin's King & Queen and going on to listen to the band in the Pavilion Grounds. Jonah's RAF trade was connected with Signals and he became stationed along the coast at a Radar Unit within easy reach of Brighton. This accounted for his presence as he was able to get home often. There is no doubt we were all dismayed at the news of Cyril, but I felt affected the worst.

Dawn broke on a new day, Whit Monday. I posted my letter to Margaret and kicked my heels doing little; in the evening I went to the church hall with some friends. One of them was playing the grand piano and when several of us gathered around it the support holding up the lid was accidentally knocked away. I dodged back to avoid being hit on the head and the tip of the lid smashed the left lens of my spectacles, leaving the frame on my nose. Frank had a good look at my eye and thought it was cut so he came home with me, and then we walked to the Sussex County Eye Hospital. It was 22.30 hours as we walked into the hospital through the sandbagged entrance and there was no waiting about. A nurse sat me in a chair and called a Sister who examined the damage and remarked "*I'm afraid you have a serious injury.*" Frank returned to my home giving them the news while at the hospital events moved fast. I was helped into a chair with a blanket, wheeled to a ward and tucked into bed. A surgeon was called in and within two hours I underwent an operation to remove a piece of glass which was deep in my eye.

It was ironic that this should happened so close to Cyril being reported missing, for here I was out of action with a bandage covering both eyes and orders not to move my head. The concern was the eye may become infected and result in its loss, as happened to an army fellow who was brought in a few days later with a piece of pebble in his eye caused by a mine exploding on the beach. He did lose his eye and to some extent this affected my thoughts at the time. Recovery was a slow business, Jonah soon visited me, I asked him to write to Margaret and he sent a further letter which I dictated. My mother kept her abreast of the situation and she came to Brighton on the 29th July by which time the bandage had been removed. I was being allowed out of the hospital in the afternoons and well able to get about. We met every day and it was fortunate that I was transferred to the RAF Hospital Halton, Bucks just a week later on the 6th August. She saw me away at the station and travelled back to Goole the day after.

The hospital at Halton was entirely for RAF casualties and I was among others who had similar injuries. We spent a lot of time around a large bowl of steaming water with wooden spoons wrapped with bandages; these were dipped in the water and held up to the eye to provide steam heat treatment. This did little for me as I still had no vision in the eye it only revealed whether what I was seeing was light or dark. I went to a garden party at Buckingham Palace while at Halton, feeling rather a fraud because I was not war wounded but no questions were asked and it was enjoyable. After eighteen days I was discharged from hospital with 14 days' sick leave and then I returned Hemswell. The C.O. drove from Bawtry to see me and we chatted in the Defence Office for two hours, I must have convinced him of my fitness for duty as he kept me on and I was back at the school. The aerodrome was non-operational while new runways were being installed so life was peaceful, and the school had altered its programme with far greater concentration on handling weapons with no strenuous exercises. However, I knew this minor disability of mine would let me down when I came to see the consultant in the months ahead and would affect my future with the Regiment.

I was sent on a gunnery course at Filey and while there on Friday, 19th November I heard from home that Cyril had now been reported "Killed in Action" and buried at Uedem, Germany.

EPILOGUE

The war was over and a few years had passed but the aftermath was very much in evidence. The dead were still vividly in everyone's memory and monuments were being erected lest those who come after should ever forget. One humbler such monument was a gift of J. W. Cooper, the headmaster of the school which Cyril and I had attended. The date was now 6th April 1949 and the brass plaque, containing the names of the old boys of the school who lost their lives during the war was being dedicated. I went to the school straight from working in London and arrived about half way through the ceremony. Walking along the corridor lined with cabinets containing sports trophies I reached the first floor hallway where a fair number of people stood by the plaque which was about to be unveiled. I joined them at the back and while I was becoming acclimatised to the vaguely familiar surroundings the names began to be read out. I froze as I heard my name – K.C. Chambers - mentioned after Cyril.

At the end, Uncle Stan and Aunt Lottie turned, expressing surprise at seeing me. They were sad eyed as we walked slowly out of the school and both almost together said *"Did you know the other Chambers who was read out?"* I shook my head, knowing full well it was my initials that went with the surname. We carried on walking to their house in Cobden Road where I left them and went on up Elm Grove to my house in Whippingham Road. Opening the door I greeted my wife Margaret with a hug and a kiss, and then turned away with tears pouring down my face. She knew where I had been and understood because she had lived the time along with me.

Maybe the spiritual force which joined Cyril and me together was determined not to be broken. In my mind it never will.

Update - March 2009

Ken married **Margaret** at Goole Parish Church on 31st July 1945. He resumed living in Brighton, together with Margaret, after being demobbed in 1946, and retired in 1982 after 32 years service with an International Oil Company. Ken and Margaret still live in the area of Brighton close to St Luke's Church.

Owen (Gurton) married **Bet**, they live in Scotland.

Phyl (Bet's sister) still resides in Brighton.

Jonah (Roland Joanes) died August 1975.

John (Bower) died December 2007 – now at rest in Spithurst Churchyard

Erne (Ernest Carey) died March 1976 – now at rest in Spithurst Churchyard

Millie (Amelia Carey) died August 1983 – now at rest in Spithurst Churchyard

Frank (Gander) married **Peggy Jones** – he died in Australia, March 1999.

Monty (Montague Tyler) served with the Commando's during the war – he died March 1991

The Padre (The Rev. Oscar Brooks) died October 1971.

Vic (Ken's brother) died in Africa, August 1991.

Wynne (Ken's sister) died January 1993.

Cyril was re-buried at the Reichswald Forest War Cemetery, Kleve, Germany. His grave is reference 1. G 7.

Lightning Source UK Ltd.
Milton Keynes UK
UKOW022228010212

186465UK00002B/38/P